PEOPLES
of
AFRICA

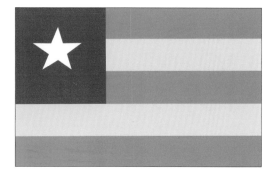

Togo

Tunisia

Uganda

Zambia

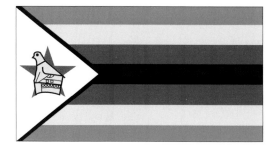

Zimbabwe

PEOPLES

of

AFRICA

Volume 10
Togo–Zimbabwe

MARSHALL CAVENDISH
NEW YORK • LONDON • TORONTO • SYDNEY

Marshall Cavendish Corporation
99 White Plains Road
Tarrytown, New York 10591-9001

Reference Edition 2003

©2001 Marshall Cavendish Corporation

Consultants:
Bryan Callahan, Department of History, Johns Hopkins University
Kevin Shillington

Pronunciation Consultant: Nancy Gratton

Contributing authors:
    Fiona Macdonald
    Elizabeth Paren
    Kevin Shillington
    Gillian Stacey
    Philip Steele

Discovery Books
    Managing Editor: Paul Humphrey
    Project Editor: Helen Dwyer
    Text Editor: Valerie J. Weber
    Design Concept: Ian Winton
    Designer: Barry Dwyer
    Cartographer: Stefan Chabluk

Marshall Cavendish
    Editorial Director: Paul Bernabeo
    Editor: Marian Armstrong

The publishers would like to thank the following for their permission to reproduce photographs:
    Corbis (Bettmann: 550, 567); Robert Estall Photo Library (Carol Beckwith / Angela Fisher: 548; David Coulson: 574); gettyone Stone (Oldrich Karasek: 544; Ian Murphy: 569); Robert Harding Picture Library (David Beatty: 538); Hutchison Library (541; John Egan: 545 top; Sarah Errington: 558; Maurice Harvey: 535 top; Juliet Highet: 545 bottom; Crispin Hughes: 551, 557; Simon McBride: 580; Sarah Murray: 537; Edward Parker: cover; Philip Wolmuth: 573); ICCE Photolibrary (Tom Skitt: 578); Christine Osborne / MEP (543, 579; Kaye Pratt: 535 bottom, 536); Panos Pictures (Fred Hoogervorst: 546, 556, 559; Caroline Penn: 534; Giacomo Pirozzi: 542, 564, 570, 572; Catherine Platt: 582; Steve Thomas: 576, 583; J. C. Tordai: 562); Still Pictures (Julio Etchart: 560, 563; Steve Lewis / Christian Aid: 581; Jorgen Schytte: 552, 553, 554, 555); Tropix Photographic Library (M. & V. Birley: 571; John Deeney: 530, 533)

(cover) A chief of the Lundu people of Cameroon.

Editor's note: Many systems of dating have been used by different cultures throughout history. *Peoples of Africa* uses B.C.E. (Before Common Era) and C.E. (Common Era) instead of B.C. (Before Christ) and A.D. (Anno Domini, "In the Year of the Lord") out of respect for the diversity of the world's peoples.

Library of Congress Cataloging-in-Publication Data

Peoples of Africa.
    p. cm.
    Includes bibliographical references and index.
    Contents: v. 1. Algeria–Botswana — v. 2. Burkina–Faso–Comoros — v. 3. Congo,
Democratic Republic of–Eritrea — v. 4. Ethiopia–Guinea — v. 5. Guinea-Bissau–Libya —
v. 6. Madagascar–Mayotte — v. 7. Morocco–Nigeria — v. 8. Réunion–Somalia — v. 9.
South Africa–Tanzania — v. 10. Togo–Zimbabwe — v. 11. Index.
    ISBN 0-7614-7158-8 (set)
    1. Ethnology—Africa—Juvenile literature. 2. Africa—History—Juvenile literature. 3.
Africa—Social life and customs—Juvenile literature. I. Marshall Cavendish Corporation.

GN645 .P33 2000
305.8'0096—dc21

                                      99-088550

    ISBN 0-7614-7158-8 (set)
    ISBN 0-7614-7168-5 (vol. 10)

Printed in Hong Kong

06   05   04   03   6   5   4   3   2

Contents

TOGO

TOGO OCCUPIES A NARROW STRIP OF LAND, stretching inland from the Gulf of Guinea, in western Africa.

Along the coast the land is flat, with sandy beaches and marshy lagoons. In the central region stands a raised plateau with high hills covered in rain forests and coffee plantations. The north is an area of flat savanna.

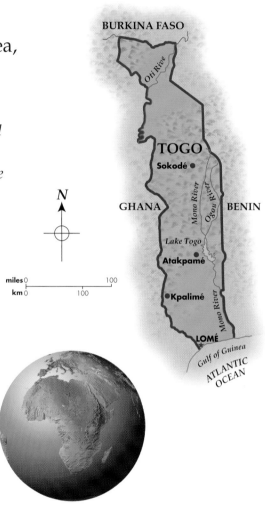

Village houses of the Moba people of northern Togo have mud-brick walls and thatched roofs. Garden plots of tall green sorghum, an edible grain, stand close by.

African Migrations and European Rivalries

So far, archaeological research has not uncovered any firm signs of settlement in Togo (TOE-goe) before around 600 B.C.E. Between 600 B.C.E. and 1100 C.E., farmers began settling in the mountains of north-central Togo. The Ewe (EH-vae) are thought to have moved into southern Togo

CLIMATE

Togo has a warm, but not extreme, tropical climate. Temperatures remain much the same year-round. Rainfall is heaviest in the hilly central region.

Average January temperature: *79°F (26°C)*
Average July temperature: *79°F (26°C)*
Average annual precipitation: *45 in. (114 cm)*

from Nigeria somewhere between the 1300s and 1600s. By the 1600s they had established themselves in the coastal region of Togo, where they met and mingled with the Mina (MEE-nah), who had recently

530

arrived from Ghana in the west. Both these peoples profited from trade with the Portuguese that began in the 1470s. During the 1700s, major migrations began into the northern parts of Togo from the region of Burkina Faso. The newcomers integrated with the existing inhabitants and today most of the peoples of northern Togo speak languages related to those of Burkina Faso.

During the mid-1800s rival European nations competed to take control of African lands. Togo became a German protectorate in 1884, although many Togolese peoples continued to fight against German rule until 1902. German settlers introduced large-scale economic developments, building railroads and roads and setting up coffee and cocoa plantations. In 1914 Great Britain and France, who were at war with Germany, took control of Togo.

When World War I ended, the League of Nations placed the western third of Togo under British protection and the eastern two-thirds under French protection. Neither Great Britain nor France put much effort into developing Togo. The British joined their share of Togo to their colony of the Gold Coast (now Ghana); the French ruled theirs as a separate state. This meant that the peoples and communities of Togo were divided. In protest Ewe peoples throughout western Africa began to campaign for a nation of their own.

In 1956 the people of West Togo voted in a referendum to join with the Gold Coast, which was preparing to become independent, as Ghana (see GHANA). France agreed to grant East Togo independence as the republic of Togo. As a

---

FACTS AND FIGURES

Official name: *République Togolaise*

Status: *Independent state*

Capital: *Lomé*

Major towns: *Sokodé, Kpalimé, Atakpamé*

Area: *21,853 square miles (56,599 square kilometers)*

Population: *4,500,000*

Population density: *206 per square mile (80 per square kilometer)*

Peoples: *Over 30 ethnic groups, of which the largest are the Ewe and Mina; others include the Kabiye, Moba, Kotokoli, Bassari, Akposo, Gurma, and Lamba*

Official language: *French*

Currency: *CFA franc*

National days: *National Liberation Day (January 13); Independence Day (April 23)*

Country's name: *Togo means "by the water" in the Ewe language.*

---

first step, in 1956 Togo became a self-governing community while remaining part of France.

Colonial Rule Ends, Independence Begins

In 1960 Togo became free of colonial rule. Sylvanus Olympio, an Ewe from the south, became the first president of Togo. In 1963 a crisis arose when Olympio refused to allow northerners who had fought in the French colonial army to join Togo's army. In response angry army leaders staged a

Time line:	Farmers settle in north-central Togo	Ewe move into southern Togo	Ewe and Mina begin trade with Portuguese	Togo becomes German protectorate
	ca. 600 B.C.E.–1100 C.E.	**ca. 1300s–1600s C.E.**	**ca. 1470s**	**1884**

coup, Olympio was killed, and coup leader Nicolas Grunitzky became the new president. In 1967 a rival leader Etienne Eyadéma, from the Kabiye (kuh-BEE-yuh) people, organized a bloodless coup. He suspended the constitution, dismissed the opposition, and set up a single-party state.

Eyadéma tightened his control on the country even further by nationalizing the important phosphate industry (used for fertilizer) and introducing an "authenticity" campaign, designed to get rid of all traces of French and German colonial rule. He abolished French names (and took a new Kabiye first name, Gnassingbe) and ordered that Kabiye and Ewe be used in primary schools instead of French. He also launched economic development projects, but many lost money or failed. Economic problems increased after world phosphate prices collapsed in the 1980s. International aid organizations gave loans to help, but they demanded major changes to government economic policy in return.

By the mid-1980s opposition to Eyadéma's rule was increasing at home. In response Eyadéma clamped down on civil and political liberties. The jails filled with political prisoners amid allegations of brutality and torture. In 1990 mass demonstrations erupted after members of an opposition group based in Ivory Coast were put on trial in Lomé (loe-MAE). To try and calm his opponents, Eyadéma legalized political parties in 1991, but protests continued.

Eyadéma promised elections, but there were many delays. Elections held in 1993 were widely seen as undemocratic because most of the opposition was in prison. An uneasy calm prevailed throughout the 1990s, with Eyadéma winning another disputed presidential election in 1998. Meanwhile, the economy suffered as the international community suspended aid because of widespread human rights violations.

Tiny Land Holds Many Ethnic Groups

Togo is a small country, yet it is home to over thirty peoples. The Ewe and Mina dominate the south.

In the countryside most Ewe are farmers, growing food, such as corn, millet, sorghum, yams, and cassava, for their own families. They also keep cattle, sheep, and goats. If they live near the coast or a river, the Ewe catch fish, using huge nets requiring fifty men to haul them in.

Traditional Ewe society was based on a system of extended families—groups of relatives who were all descended from a common ancestor. The eldest man was the head of each family, commanding obedience and respect. Land belonged to family groups, not individuals, and could not be sold. Families worked the land together and shared the resulting crops. Today, as people move away from their home villages to seek work or an education, these family groups are no longer so important. Land is bought and sold, and individuals increasingly rely on their own efforts for money to buy food. However, regional chiefs have the right to hold courts that control ancient customs,

Togo divided between Great Britain and France	West Togo joins Ghana; East Togo becomes independent state	Etienne Eyadéma takes power in coup	Phosphate prices fall; economic problems; human rights violations	Eyadéma remains in power; human rights violations continue; foreign aid stopped
1914	**1960**	**1967**	**1980s**	**1990s**

A Lamba boy from northern Togo stands surrounded by dry savanna grasses. He wears a wide-brimmed hat of braided straw to shade his head from the hot sun.

for export. Both groups were given educational preference in colonial times and dominated the civil service as clerks, junior administrators, and teachers. This system caused tension between northern and southern peoples.

The Kabiye people live in the mountains of north-central Togo around the town of Sokodé (soe-KOE-dae). In the extreme north some peoples such as the Gurma (GOOR-mah) and the Moba (MOE-bah) speak languages of a group called Gur, while others such as the Lamba (LAHM-buh) speak languages of the Tem family.

The Kabiye and some northern peoples are mostly subsistence farmers. The Kabiye are skilled at growing crops in a very harsh environment, the dry, savanna region. They grow millet and yams to feed themselves and cotton to sell.

Famous traders and weavers, the Muslim Kotokoli (koe-toe-KOE-lee) people arrived in northern Togo from Mali in the 1800s. They have a strict code of manners; Kotokoli people bow to each other upon meeting and sometimes children kneel before their elders. Men wear long, flowing robes and skullcaps, while the women wear similar robes with transparent scarves over their head and shoulders.

The Bassari (buh-SAH-ree), another northern people, have a tradition of ironworking, and some of their festivals are marked by fire dances. Participants brave the flames in a trance, hoping to communicate with spirits.

All of Togo's peoples speak their own languages. The official language, French, is

for example, animal-grazing rights. Ordinary people still listen respectfully to the opinions of village and regional chiefs.

There are strong links between the Ewe and Mina peoples in Togo and peoples who speak related languages across the borders in Ghana and Benin (see GHANA and BENIN). Since the Germans arrived in Togo in the late nineteenth century, the Ewe and Mina have also worked as commercial farmers, growing coffee, cocoa, and cotton

Let's Talk Ewe

Ewe and Mina are the most widely spoken languages in Togo. Mina is closely related to Ewe; both belong to the Twi language family.

ngdi — *hello, good day*
(ehng-DEE)

woe zo — *welcome*
(wah ZOE)

hede nyuie — *good-bye*
(huh-DAEN WEE)

taflatse — *please*
(tuh-FLAHT-suh)

nko wode? — *what is your name?*
(uhn-KWOE-dae)

used for government business, in secondary schools and universities, and by the educated elite.

Almost three-quarters of the people in Togo follow *vodu* (voe-DOO; see BENIN), which combines Christian and African beliefs. They worship the Christian God as well as many local gods and spirits. Like many other African peoples, they honor the spirits of their dead ancestors and believe that their ancestors have the power to harm or help them. Religious practices include calling up spirits by dancing, chanting, and falling into a trance. Many shrines with carved statues of spirits or powerful forces stand beside busy roads or in

marketplaces. People leave offerings of food in front of these shrines, asking the spirit powers for help.

About 15 percent of the population are Muslim. There is no strict division of belief across the country, but vodu and Christianity are more common in the south, while Islam is followed in the center and north.

A Nation Torn Apart

Togo is a divided society. Today many Ewe are exiles in Ghana and France because they oppose President Eyadéma and fear for their safety if they return home. Poverty and distrust of politicians—leading to a sense of hopelessness about achieving anything by peaceful, legal means—has also led to a rapid increase in crime.

Children are supposed to go to school for at least six years, but only 75 percent of elementary-school-age children and 25 percent of secondary-school-age children attend. The rest stay at home to help their parents earn a living. As a result, only two-thirds of men over fifteen and only one-third of all women can read and write.

Togolese people often ask vodu practitioners for advice. Here, cowrie shells are being used for fortune-telling. The future is predicted from the pattern made by the shells.

534

These village men have joined together in a patrol to protect their homes, families, and neighborhood roads from attack by armed bandit gangs that roam the countryside.

Students who do stay in school often complete their education by going to the university in Lomé or studying at universities and colleges in France.

There are hospitals in most big cities and medical treatment is available in many towns, but health care is not free, and many people are too poor to pay for medicines. Average life expectancy is forty-eight years for men and fifty years for women.

As elsewhere in western Africa, houses are usually single story and are arranged around a courtyard. Today they are made from concrete and tin, but many older houses, with walls made of mud-and-straw bricks and roofs of grass, remain in villages and country towns. Northern houses often have round granaries made of sun-dried mud nearby to store millet and corn.

Rural health workers explain to villagers the dangers of catching a killer disease, such as sleeping sickness, from flies that live on riverbanks.

A Poor Economy

Togo is a poor country. About one-third of the population cannot earn enough for adequate housing, clothes, and health care. The government is in debt to foreign companies and organizations.

The economy of Togo is based on farming. Togo has been self-sufficient in food since 1982, and around 65 percent of the working population earns their living from the land. Large-scale plantations produce coffee, cocoa, and cotton for export.

Togo's few industries are based on the country's main natural resources: phosphates in the south and iron ore in the north. The main industrial products are fertilizers, cement, handicrafts, textiles, and beverages. Factories process and pack farm produce for export.

A woman trader selling smoked fish in Lomé, the capital. Throughout Togo most market traders are women who control the buying and selling of locally produced foods.

Foufou and Sauce

Although a lot of people in Togo are poor, few go hungry. The basis of a meal consists of a starchy food such as rice; fluffy pellets of boiled millet; cassava root; *foufou* (FOO-foo), which are mashed yams; or *akoumé* (ah-KOO-mae), which is a dough made of crushed millet, corn, or plantains. All are served with sauce, which is a vegetable stew with peanuts or a little meat. Locally grown foods include okra, squash, tomatoes, eggplants, and beans. Meats include grilled chicken and goat. Snails are also eaten. Smoked foods and dishes flavored with hot chili peppers are popular. Fish can be smoked, spiced, and baked or cooked in sauce. For dessert there are

tropical fruits, such as pineapples, bananas, papayas, guavas, and mangoes. To drink, *tchakpallo* (chahk-PAH-loe), millet beer, is a favorite with northerners; in the south, villagers make palm wine and *sodabe* (soe-DAH-bae), a palm spirit.

Celebrations, Crafts, and Music

Soccer and wrestling are favorite sports. In July the Kabiye people hold the Evala festival, which marks the time when young boys become adult men. It is celebrated with wresting matches, often televised. Wrestlers coat their bodies with slippery shea butter, a natural plant oil, so opponents cannot grip them easily. Large crowds also gather to see traditional dancing at local festivals.

In September the Ewe hold the Agbogbozan (ahg-BAWG-boe-zahn) festival, which celebrates Ewe culture and identity and promotes the idea of uniting the Ewe people in one state.

Also in September, the Mina people celebrate the Yékéyéké (yaek-YAE-kee) festival, which lasts four whole days. People make offerings of money and food to various gods, such as Egou, protector-god of the Mina, and ask to be blessed by traditional priests. Animals are sacrificed, and a grand ceremony is held when the color of the coming year's sacred stone (used in religious rituals) is revealed. Its color is chosen by the local people and acts as an omen for the coming year, for example, blue means plentiful rain while red warns of a dangerous year ahead.

A Muslim festival in Sokodé in the northern region combines Islamic and local African elements. It is called Adossa (ah-DAW-sah), or the Knife Festival, and it marks the Prophet Muhammad's birthday. Men drink a potion prepared by a Muslim religious leader, then dance in public, cutting each other with knives. The potion is said to protect them from serious harm.

The Togolese have long been skilled wood-carvers. Many rain forest trees produce beautiful, richly colored wood, which artisans have used to create fine statues, masks, and other objects over the centuries. Village artisans also produce decorated calabashes and leather work. Primarily male weavers produce narrow strips of brightly colored *keta* (KEH-tah) cloth, usually of cotton, using hand looms. These are sewn together to make a striped cloth used for wall hangings or worn wrapped loosely around the body. This cloth closely resembles the more famous *kente* (KEHN-tee) cloth produced by the Ashanti people of Ghana (see GHANA). Togolese women wear clothes of very brightly printed cotton fabric.

Many kinds of music are popular in Togo. Singers and bands perform in both modern and older styles. Kabiye musicians play unusual instruments such as stone xylophones and water flutes. Drums are played at public occasions, and drumming is often accompanied by dancing and singing. In the past, songs were also used to express hostilities against rivals; at a gathering known as a *halo* (HAH-loe), rival villagers sang insulting songs to each other. Today songs mostly showcase singers' skills.

This shop close to the Lomé market sells brightly colored cotton batik cloth. It takes nearly 20 feet (6 meters) of cloth to make a robe in Togolese style.

TUNISIA

TUNISIA IS THE NORTHERNMOST COUNTRY
IN AFRICA. It borders the
Mediterranean Sea.

*Tunisia's sandy coastline stretches for
about 800 miles (1,287 kilometers).
High, jagged mountains stand in the
north, while in the central region lie
high, dusty plains. In the south there is
a vast salty, sandy desert with salt lakes.
There is only one permanent river, the
Medjerda, in the north.*

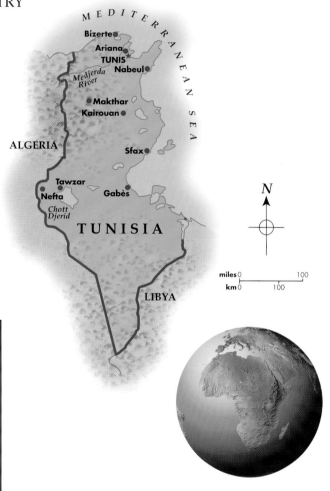

CLIMATE

The north has mild, rainy winters and hot, dry
summers. In the south it is hot and dry year-
round, with strong winds from the Sahara Desert.

Average January temperature: *45°F (7°C)*

Average July temperature: *90°F (32°C)*

Average annual precipitation:
   in the north: *16 in. (41 cm)*
   in the south: *6 in. (15 cm)*

*Berber women harvesting grain by
hand near Makthar (MAK-tuhr)
in the northwest. Berber women
are free to work outside the
home, unlike many other women
in northern Africa.*

From the Berbers to the French

The first inhabitants of Tunisia (too-NEE-zhuh) were Berbers (BUHR-buhrs), the earliest known people of northern Africa. From the 1100s to 100s B.C.E., groups of Phoenicians, from the eastern Mediterranean, set up trading colonies along the Tunisian coast. The greatest of these colonies, Carthage, grew into a rich and powerful city. In 105 B.C.E. the Romans conquered Tunisia and built cities and colonies. Roman rule lasted until the 400s C.E., when invaders from central Europe took over Roman lands. They were soon followed by Byzantines from present-day Turkey.

During the 600s, Muslim soldiers from Arabia conquered all of northern Africa. To help spread Islam, Muslim rulers of Tunisia encouraged Arab tribes to migrate from Egypt. Although they were defeated and ruled by Arabs, Berbers remained the majority of the population for many hundreds of years.

In 1062 Saharan Berber Muslims conquered Tunisia and Morocco and established the Almoravid dynasty. A century later, the Almoravid lands were conquered by the Almohad dynasty from Morocco, who divided the empire: Tunisia became part of Ifriqiyya (ih-FREEK-yah), ruled by the Hafsid dynasty. (Today's name *Africa* is a modern version of the old name for Tunisia and the nearby lands.)

In 1578 the Turks captured Tunis, bringing it under their Ottoman Empire. The Ottoman governors used Tunis as a base to raid European shipping.

In the mid–nineteenth century, Great Britain and France forced the Ottoman governor to end piracy. France invaded in 1881 and declared Tunisia a French protectorate two years later. French settlers arrived and over the next fifty years they took control of the best land.

From the beginning, Tunisians protested against French rule, but the French government refused to give Tunisians any political rights. In 1934 Habib Bourguiba became head of the nationalist Néo-Destour (New Constitution) Party. His

FACTS AND FIGURES

Official name: *Al Jumhuriyah at Tunisiyah (Republic of Tunisia)*

Status: *Independent state*

Capital: *Tunis*

Major towns: *Sfax, Ariana, Bizerte, Gabès*

Area: *63,378 square miles (164,149 square kilometers)*

Population: *9,500,000*

Population density: *150 per square mile (58 per square kilometer)*

Peoples: *98 percent Berber, Arab, and mixed Berber-Arab; some Europeans*

Official language: *Arabic*

Currency: *Dinar*

National days: *Independence Day (March 20); Youth Day (March 21); Republic Day (July 25); Anniversary of Ben Ali's Takeover (November 7)*

Country's name: *The country's name comes from the city of Tunis, which takes its name from the nearby lake.*

Time line:	Phoenician traders encounter Berber inhabitants of region	Country under Roman rule	Muslim rule	Ottoman rule	Tunisia becomes French protectorate
	1100s–100s B.C.E.	**105 B.C.E.–400s C.E.**	**600s–1578 C.E.**	**1578–1883**	**1883**

campaigns soon built up opposition to France. In 1949 he led nonviolent freedom protests, which led to counter-demonstrations by European settlers in Tunisia against the independence campaigners. Protesters on both sides turned to violence, and the threat of civil war hung in the air. In 1954 France agreed to self-rule for Tunisia, and in 1956 the country became fully independent.

The Years since Independence

In 1957 Tunisia became a republic, with Bourguiba as president. He aimed to maintain links with (and receive aid from) France and other Western states and encouraged economic development and modernization, with great success. To improve conditions for women, he introduced a law that banned polygamy and opposed *hijab* (hee-ZHAHB), the Muslim head covering. He also outraged Muslims by encouraging workers to give up the Ramadan fast in order to increase their productivity. Bourguiba's government also took over all French-owned lands. In 1964 Tunisia became a one-party state under the renamed Destour Socialist Party.

By the 1970s Muslim opposition to Bourguiba was growing. In response, he imprisoned many political opponents and cracked down severely on strikers pressing for better pay and work conditions and the right to practice traditional Muslim customs. All this strengthened the opposition's resolve. In 1981 Bourguiba announced multiparty elections but refused to let the leading Islamic opposition party, the Islamic Tendency Movement, take part. Its leaders were imprisoned, and there were accusations of vote rigging.

During the 1980s Bourguiba's rule became increasingly autocratic and out of touch with ordinary citizens. In 1987, after a show trial, he called for the leaders of the Islamic opposition to be executed. This led to a political crisis and fears of revolution. Zine al-Abidine Ben Ali, minister of the interior, asked doctors to declare Bourguiba (eighty-three years old by then) unfit for public duties. Bourguiba was held in detention, then retired.

As the new leader, Ben Ali tried to make peace with the Islamic opposition. He promised multiparty elections, though the leading Islamic party, renamed Al-Nahda (Renaissance), was still banned. He released political prisoners and reduced police powers. Encouraged, some political exiles returned. In 1989 elections were held, but some accusations of vote rigging still arose. The leaders of Al-Nahda could not take part, but many of its supporters campaigned as independents and were elected. In response, the government alleged that Islamic leaders were plotting revolution and sent them back to prison.

Further elections took place during the 1990s, and each time, the government claimed 99 percent support. Many Tunisians—and foreign onlookers—do not believe this claim, and the political situation remains tense. However, Tunisia's economy is thriving, and many people are content to let the present government stay in power.

Independence with Habib Bourguiba as prime minister	One-party state under Destour Socialist Party	Bourguiba removed from office	President Ben Ali introduces reforms; political prisoners released	Ben Ali remains in power; Islamic activists suppressed
1956	**1964**	**1987**	**1988**	**1988–2000**

Muslim worshipers enter a mosque built above the tomb of a Muslim holy man. The sites where respected Muslim teachers are buried often become places of prayer.

Peoples of Tunisia

Most Tunisians are of mixed ancestry, descended from Berbers, Arabs, and Spanish and Turkish Muslims. All speak Arabic and many also speak French. A few Berber villages remain in the southeast and in the western mountains, but their language is dying out fast. Small communities of Europeans and Jews also live in coastal cities. The land is very densely populated in the north, especially around Tunis, and very sparsely settled in the south.

Almost everyone living in Tunisia is Muslim. Moderate observance of Islam plays an important part in all aspects of Tunisian life, and the Tunisian code of law is based on Islamic values, as well as French civil law. The city of Kairouan (ker-WAHN), in the north, is one of the holiest cities in the Islamic world. There are also long traditions in Tunisia of Sufism, which is a form of Muslim mysticism, and of maraboutism, or intense respect for religious teachers or Muslim holy men.

Outwardly Western, Inwardly Traditional

In many ways, Tunisian society is Westernized and very modern. Most people no longer work on small family farms but in big-city stores, offices, and hotels. For entertainment, people watch television, go to movies, watch soccer and handball, or, especially men, go to restaurants and cafés to meet friends, smoke, read newspapers, and play backgammon. Many people live in modern apartment buildings built of concrete and glass instead of older low-rise courtyard homes, although a farm or village may have a jumble of newer concrete buildings alongside older homes built of mud brick.

However, Tunisian people still maintain many Islamic values and long-established customs. Close-knit family groups are still very important for most Tunisians, old and young. Most choose to maintain conventional Muslim standards of dress and public decency. Older-style Tunisian clothes for men and women are long loose robes. Today many Tunisians wear European-style clothes in the latest fashions, but they take care not to wear their skirts or pants too short or too tight or to show too much bare skin. Public displays of physical affection (except between parents and children) are frowned upon.

People living in the countryside primarily work on farms. Irrigated land provides the dates and fruit for which Tunisia is famous, and cattle are raised for leather. Other country dwellers work in phosphate mining and in the oil fields. However, unemployment is high in the countryside.

Many desert dwellers in Tunisia live at oases, growing crops such as dates, bananas, melons, olives, pomegranates, figs, oranges, lemons, beans, cucumbers, and tomatoes. Small numbers of nomadic Berbers—the Tuareg (TWAHR-ehg)—and Arabic-speaking Bedouin peoples live in the Sahara Desert, trading and searching for pasture for their livestock (see ALGERIA, EGYPT, and LIBYA). Tourism is an important industry; many desert dwellers run hotels, sell souvenirs, take tourists to see nomad camps (which are usually fake), and offer camel rides to visitors.

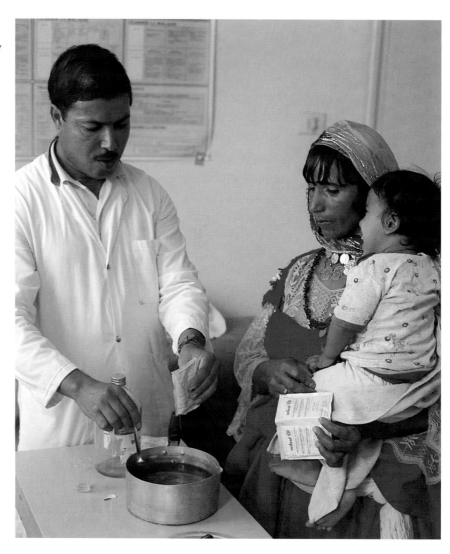

A Tunisian doctor shows a Berber mother how to prepare an oral rehydration solution, a lifesaving mixture of boiled water, sugar, and salt, given to babies with diarrhea.

Health and Education

Most Tunisians have a varied diet, access to clean water and drainage systems, and decent housing. The government health and social security system includes free medical care. As a result of all this, the average life expectancy is high: sixty-eight years for men and seventy years for women. Most families are small, with two or three children.

Tunisia also has a fairly high standard of education. Almost eight out of every ten men, and about six out of every ten women, can read and write. Primary and secondary schooling, which the state provides for free, is compulsory. There are also higher education colleges and universities.

A Wealthy Economy

Tunisia is one of the most prosperous countries in Africa. Its economy is based on farming, mining, and manufacturing. Farmers, who live mostly in the north, grow olives, dates, fruit, almonds, and sugar beets and raise poultry and beef and dairy cattle. Miners quarry for phosphates, iron ore, lead, zinc, and salt and drill for oil and petroleum. Factory workers produce clothing, footwear, and food and drink. However, growing environmental problems, including water shortages, chemical pollution, deforestation, overgrazing, desertification, and soil erosion, may affect future economic growth.

There is a booming film industry. Tunisia's dramatic landscape and interesting old buildings have been used as a backdrop for many feature films, including *Star Wars*. The tourist industry is increasingly important, and it is the biggest employer in Tunisia today.

With its long coastline, Tunisia has several important ports. The European Union is Tunisia's main trading partner. Tunisia exports mainly oil and gas, textiles, farm produce, phosphates, and chemicals.

Foods—Traditional and European

Tunisian foods include meat and vegetable soups and stews, such as *lablabi* (lah-BLAH-bee), a chickpea soup, *kammounia* (kah-MOON-yah), a meat stew with cumin, and *shakshuka* (SHAHKSH-kah), a vegetable stew with tomato sauce. Many of these dishes are strongly spiced with chilis, peppers, and herbs. Favorite snacks are *briq* (BREEK), a pastry with meat and egg filling, and *ojja* (OE-jah), a vegetable and

Tunisia is famous for producing fine dates. These dates are growing at the oasis town of Nefta (NEF-tuh), which has some of the largest date-palm plantations in Tunisia.

Ma'amoul B'Tamer (*mah-MOOL bi-TAH-mer*): Date Cookies

You will need:

9 ounces (255 grams) of dried dates
1 cup (240 milliliters) of boiling water
4 ¹/₂ ounces (128 grams) of flour
4 ¹/₂ ounces (128 grams) of cornstarch
9 ounces (255 grams) of butter or
*   margarine*
4 ¹/₂ ounces (128 grams) of sugar
optional: 1 to 2 tablespoons of
*   milk, cold water, or rose water*

Chop dates finely and put them in a heat-proof bowl. Pour boiling water over them, and let stand for thirty minutes until dates are soft.

To make cookie dough, beat sugar and butter together until light and fluffy. Mix flour and cornstarch together, and stir gently into the butter mixture. If the cookie mixture is too stiff, add milk, water, or rose water.

To add date filling, take small lumps of the cookie dough, about the size of walnuts, and gently shape into balls. Using your thumb, make a hollow in each ball. Almost fill the hollow with dates, then pinch the tops of the hollow together to cover the dates. Place filled balls on a greased baking sheet. Bake at 325°F (160°C) for about 20 to 25 minutes, until pale golden yellow. Do not overcook. Makes approximately twelve cookies.

egg mixture. Fish, often freshly grilled, is eaten along the coast. Sweet pastries, such as *makhroud* (mahk-ROOD), a cake made from dates and semolina, and almond biscuits, together with fresh fruits, provide dessert. Oranges, pomegranates, bananas, melons, and grapes all grow in Tunisia. Tea, coffee, and soft drinks are popular. Many stores and restaurants sell Western-style foods, such as pizza, pasta, and cola, plus French-style baguette sandwiches.

Shoppers can buy tasty snacks from a street stall at Nabeul (nab-YOOL), a busy seaside resort on the northeast coast. Favorite snacks include both sweet and savory pastries.

Winding newly spun woolen thread on a large, foot-powered wheel. Finished wool lies in heaps close by, ready to use for making rugs.

The Craft of Carpet Making

Carpet making is Tunisia's best-known craft. Carpets and rugs are made in many different patterns and styles, using different techniques. *Mergoums* (maer-GOOMS) and kilims are woven carpets with a flat pile (surface). Mergoums are brightly colored in reds, blues, and purples; kilims are woven in muted colors, using ancient Berber designs. Often patterned with geometric designs, Kairouan carpets are made by tying millions of tiny knots onto a woven backing. *Guetiffa* (geh-TEE-fah) are knotted carpets made by Berber artisans; they are thick, fluffy, and the natural cream color of sheep's wool. The government runs a quality-control project to maintain high standards and preserve carpet-making skills.

Bright, patterned rugs for sale are displayed in the marketplace at Tawzar (TAW-zuh), a town on the edge of the desert in far western Tunisia.

545

UGANDA

UGANDA LIES ON THE EQUATOR, occupying plateau lands in eastern Africa.

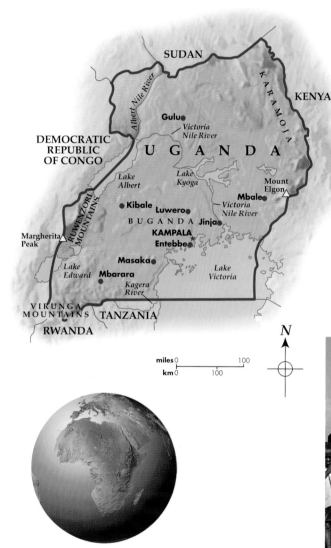

The south is a land of red soil with lush, green crops. Extensive forests grow in the west. In central and northern regions lies dusty savanna that gives way to semidesert in the northeast.

In western Uganda is a plateau fringed by the volcanic Virunga Mountains and the Ruwenzori Mountains. These rise to 16,763 feet (5,106 meters) at Margherita Peak. Uganda's mountains drain into wetlands and a series of lakes that feed the Nile River.

Schoolchildren take part in a tree-planting project near Kibale (kih-BAH-lee) in western Uganda. Uganda has suffered from severe deforestation, but President Yoweri Museveni has made care for the environment a priority.

CLIMATE

Uganda's weather is generally hot and sunny, with fresh breezes. The temperature remains fairly constant throughout the year. Rainfall is heaviest between March and May.

Average January temperature: *74°F (23°C)*

Average July temperature: *70°F (21°C)*

Average annual precipitation: *46 in. (117 cm)*

Between the Lakes

In ancient times great areas of Uganda (yoo-GAHN-dah) were densely forested. Through these equatorial forests wandered small bands of people who hunted wild animals, fished in the lakes and rivers, and gathered wild roots and berries for food.

Between three and two thousand years ago, forest farmers from the Cameroon region began to expand their settlements southward and eastward toward central and eastern Africa. They spoke a group of languages known as Bantu (BAN-too). In the lake region of eastern Africa, the soil was fertile and water abundant. Here, the Bantu-speakers met other people from whom they learned the skills of cattle herding and crop cultivation. By the 300s B.C.E. Bantu smiths were smelting iron ore to produce high quality iron for axes and other tools. This technology enabled them to clear large areas of forest and plant crops. As their forest environment disappeared, the bands of hunter-gatherers retreated westward.

By 1000 C.E. Bantu farmers in ever-increasing numbers were settling on the shores of Lake Victoria and growing plantains as their chief crop. They were grouped into clans (people descended from a common ancestor) and ruled by chiefs.

New peoples began to migrate into the savanna grasslands of northern Uganda too. They came from the Nile Valley, in what is now Sudan, and from Ethiopia. Their lives revolved around raising and raiding cattle. They were less tightly governed than the Bantu chiefdoms, but in

FACTS AND FIGURES

Official name: *Republic of Uganda*

Status: *Independent state*

Capital: *Kampala*

Major towns: *Jinja, Masaka, Mbale, Mbarara, Entebbe, Gulu*

Area: *91,134 square miles (236,037 square kilometers)*

Population: *22,800,000*

Population density: *250 per square mile (97 per square kilometer)*

Peoples: *17 percent Ganda; 8 percent Iteso; 8 percent Nyankole; 8 percent Soga; 7 percent Chiga; 6 percent Lango; 6 percent Nyoro; 6 percent Rwanda; 5 percent Gisu; 4 percent Acholi; 4 percent Lugbara; 3 percent Toro; 2 percent Adhola; 2 percent Alur; 2 percent Karamojong; 1 percent Kakwa; 1 percent European, Asian, or Arab descent; about 27 other ethnic groups make up the remaining 10 percent*

Official language: *English*

Currency: *Uganda shilling*

National day: *Independence Day (October 9)*

Country's name: *The name* Uganda *is the Swahili version of Buganda, the kingdom of the Ganda people.*

Uganda the two cultures met and traded. They developed economic and political relationships, which the herders often dominated. New small states began to develop, some including both herders and farmers.

There is no written history of this early period, only names that have been passed down in tales and folklore. These refer to a

Time line:	Hunter-gatherers in forests; possible beginnings of Bantu settlements	Bantu peoples perfect iron smelting, move in to clear forests	Increasing Bantu settlement around Lake Victoria; herders move into savanna from north
	ca. 1000 B.C.E.	**ca. 300 B.C.E.**	**ca. 1000 C.E.**

people called the Tembuzi (tehm-BOO-zee), of whom little is known. They were revered as gods and were led by a figure called Ruhanga (roo-AHNG-gah). The Chwezi (CHWAE-zee) people also feature as divine beings in the myths and legends of Uganda, but they must have been a historical people—probably cattle herders migrating southward from Ethiopia. Their period in Uganda is associated with sites such as Bigo, in the west, where there are massive earthworks. By 1500 most Chwezi seem to have migrated or been pushed southward.

Lakeshore Kingdoms

By the 1500s a kingdom called Bunyoro (boon-YOE-roe), located in the north in dry savanna country, had become powerful. Other smaller states developed as Bunyoro thrived. The kingdoms that proved to be the most powerful were Bunyoro itself, Karagwe (kuh-RAHG-wae; in the south, on the western shores of Lake Victoria), and Buganda, the home of the Ganda (GAN-duh) people (which includes the lush northwestern shores of the lake).

During the 1700s Buganda became the most powerful kingdom in the region, and in the 1800s it began conquering large areas of neighboring territory. The country was ruled by a king whose title was *kabaka* (kah-BAH-kah). His rule was absolute; he had powers of life and death over his subjects. Life at the royal court was marked by councils, by rituals of drumming, dancing, and music, by feasts, and the smoking of tobacco. A fire burned continuously outside the royal residence and was only extinguished when the kabaka died. Buganda had a fleet of long war canoes patrolling Lake Victoria and an army of

The ancient and once powerful Bugandan monarchy still exists. At his coronation in 1993, Ronald Mutebi of Buganda is carried shoulder high by members of the Buffalo clan.

Rise of Bunyoro, Karagwe, Buganda, and several smaller states	Buganda kingdom dominates region	Arab traders arrive	Christian missionaries arrive	Anglo-German agreement defines area of Uganda as British territory
1500s–1600s	1700s–1800s	1840s	1877	1890

several thousand men. The Ganda built very large, fine thatched homes and mastered many crafts.

The land between the lakes was entirely cut off from the outside world. Only in the 1840s and 1850s did Muslim Arab traders from the east and north get through to Uganda. Elephant ivory from Uganda was traded for imported guns and textiles. In the 1860s British explorers also entered the region.

Christian missionaries arrived in 1877, but they did not bring peace and harmony. Many new Christians were put to death by the kabaka of Buganda in 1886, and in 1892 a civil war broke out between Protestant and Catholic converts in Buganda.

The Protectorate

Buganda remained by far the most dominant Ugandan kingdom, but by now the real power lay with outsiders. Arab traders were eager to gain commercial control of Uganda, and Europeans were seizing control of great areas of Africa. A commercial corporation, the British East Africa Company, made treaties with the kingdoms of Buganda, Ankole (AHNG-koe-lae), and Toro (TOE-roe) in 1877, and in 1890 the Germans also made a treaty with Buganda. An Anglo-German agreement signed later that year settled the boundaries between the two European powers in eastern Africa; north of the Kagera (kah-GAE-rah) River became British (Uganda). Four years later the British government made Uganda a protectorate. This meant that Great Britain controlled the territory as a colony but the royal authority of the Bugandan kabaka and other regional kings was kept intact. In 1903 the British introduced cotton as a cash crop.

Indian workers helped build a railroad link from Mombasa, in Kenya, and soon many Indians were establishing stores and businesses in Uganda. British colonial policy toward local peoples was to educate the Ganda and employ them in the civil service. Peoples from the north, such as the Acholi (ah-CHOE-lee), were recruited into the army. The fostering of ethnic divisions in this way caused many of Uganda's modern problems.

By 1921 a legislative council governed the protectorate, but it was 1945 before any Ugandans were even appointed to serve as council members. In 1953 the Bugandan kabaka, Mutesa II, demanded separate independence for his own homeland and was exiled by the British for opposing the official policy. Mutesa was allowed to return under a compromise agreement in 1955.

Independence and Terror

Self-government was achieved in 1958, and full independence came in 1962. Uganda remained a single nation but with a federal system of government. The elected prime minister was Milton Obote, whose Uganda People's Congress brought together various political parties and factions. Mutesa II became the president in name only and soon quarreled with Obote, whose aim was to create a one-party socialist state. In 1967 Obote, now president, ended the

British declare Uganda a protectorate	Legislative council established	Africans appointed to legislative council	Internal self-government	Full independence; Uganda People's Congress wins election; Milton Obote elected prime minister
1894	**1921**	**1945**	**1958**	**1962**

549

regional monarchies and banned all opposition in 1969.

Two years later Major-General Idi Amin overthrew Obote. The Asians had long dominated businesses and Uganda's economy. This was resented by many Africans, so, without warning, Amin expelled all Asians and seized their assets.

Amin also turned on the Africans themselves, murdering and torturing all opponents. He began a program of genocide against the Acholi and Lango (LANG-goe) peoples, who had supported Obote. He looted international, national, and personal assets and appointed his friends in the army as regional tyrants. During this reign of terror, some 300,000 Ugandans may have been murdered.

Amin started to claim territory from neighboring Kenya and Tanzania and in 1978 went to war with the latter. In 1979 Tanzanian troops retaliated by invading Uganda and joined with the Uganda National Liberation Front, a coalition of Ugandan exiles and dissidents. Amin fled the country.

The wide variety of political groups that had opposed Amin now argued about how to move forward. In 1980 Obote returned and was declared president after elections that were widely believed to have been rigged. Consequently he failed to bring unity or economic stability, and violence broke out in many regions.

In 1981 Yoweri Museveni and his National Resistance Army (NRA) began a four-year guerrilla war to overthrow Obote.

President Idi Amin salutes, weighed down with the medals he awarded himself. His rule of terror and genocide from 1971 to 1979 was a national and international tragedy.

By 1985 the NRA controlled a large part of the country, and in July that year Obote was ousted by the army. The coup was led by Acholi troops from the north. An Acholi, supreme military commander Tito Okello, became head of state. He negotiated and reached an agreement with Museveni, but neither side trusted the other and fighting continued. At this point the NRA had the upper hand, and in January 1986 Museveni's army captured Kampala (kahm-PAH-lah).

Idi Amin overthrows Obote, start of reign of terror	Asians expelled	Tanzania invades and helps overthrow Amin	Elections return Obote as president	Guerrillas of NRA led by Yoweri Museveni oppose Obote
1971	**1972**	**1979**	**1980**	**1981–1985**

Museveni's Uganda

Museveni, the NRA leader, became the new president in 1986. He proved to be a pragmatic leader, who quickly gained international confidence and won admiration and loans from the World Bank and the International Monetary Fund. Museveni set about diversifying the economy, making sure that it was not too dependent on any one cash crop.

Ugandan Asian fathers and sons pose outside a Hindu temple in Kampala. Idi Amin expelled Asians from Uganda in the 1970s, but some have now returned.

Gradually life in Uganda began to improve. Some expelled Asian business people began to return to Kampala and Jinja (JIN-jah). In 1993 the regional monarchies were restored.

Museveni has faced attempted coups and rebellions in many regions since he became president. In the north there has been a long-standing war with the Lord's Resistance Army (LRA), a guerrilla movement that bases its claim to power on mystical spiritual rites that are believed to make fighters invincible. The LRA has kidnapped many children and forced them to fight as soldiers. Museveni has accused the Sudanese government of supporting the LRA and another northern guerrilla group, the West Nile Bank Front. The Sudanese claim, in turn, that Uganda supports the southern rebels fighting in their country (see SUDAN). In southwestern Uganda

another anti-Museveni rebellion began in 1997 by fighters calling themselves the Allied Democratic Forces.

Thus, although Uganda is not yet a country at peace, it has changed greatly since the days of Idi Amin, and basic human rights have been restored. Museveni and the NRM generally have the support of most people.

Free and fair elections for a constitutional assembly were held in 1994. The assembly drew up a new constitution that proposed that political parties should not be allowed for at least another five years. This was approved by referendum in 1995. The following year elections were held on a nonparty basis, and Museveni was elected president by an overwhelming majority. A further referendum on the future of party politics is scheduled for the year 2000.

General Tito Okello overthrows Obote	NRA forces Okello to flee; Museveni becomes president; Asians begin to return	Monarchies reinstated	Museveni wins in presidential election	Allied Democratic Forces rebel
1985	**1986**	**1993**	**1996**	**1997**

A woman holds a basket of tea leaves freshly picked from bushes on a plantation in the Jinja district of southeastern Uganda. Tea is one of Uganda's biggest exports.

A Fertile Land

Uganda is a country with fertile land, adequate rainfall, and mineral resources. All it needs is peace in order to recover and develop.

Eight out of ten Ugandan workers are farmers. Coffee is the chief cash crop, followed by tea, cotton, and sugarcane. Foods grown principally for local markets and the home include bananas, potatoes, peanuts, sweet potatoes, the root crop cassava, beans, and grains such as millet, sorghum, corn, and rice. Cattle are the most common form of livestock, but many people also keep goats. The lakes are a great source of fish and the forests provide timber.

Mining produces gold, tin, tungsten, copper, and graphite, while limestone is quarried. The chief industries manufacture cement, textiles, footwear, soap, and fertilizers and process sugar and other foods. Brewing and hide tanning are also major industries. Uganda's hydroelectric projects provide nearly all of the country's power.

Uganda has a relatively good network of surfaced roads between the capital and major towns. Unsurfaced roads and dirt tracks cover more remote areas. Most public transportation is by bus or by *matatu* (muh-TAH-too), the shared taxi bus popular all over eastern Africa.

Everyday Life

Only 15 percent of Ugandans live in towns. Kampala and other chief centers of population include colonial period buildings, often whitewashed with rust-red grooved-iron roofs, modern hotels and offices built in recent years, cathedrals, mosques, and the Hindu or Sikh temples raised by the Ugandan Asian community in the pre-Amin days. The traditional building skills of the Ganda can be seen at the Kasubi tombs on the outskirts of Kampala, where magnificent structures of reed thatch and timber, with hangings of bark cloth, commemorate past kabakas of Buganda. They contain ancient weapons and former possessions of kabakas, such as the royal board game of *wari* (WEHR-ee). Out in the country, trails lead to small homes dotted among green banana trees

552

and plots of vegetables. In many areas the homes are built in a traditional pattern, often circular with a thatched roof.

Food is mostly simple—a balance of basic starchy food such as a millet porridge called *busera* (BOOS-rah) or cornmeal bread with a vegetable relish or a pot of stew with vegetables such as cabbage or pumpkin. Chicken, beef, and fish may be stewed or grilled. *Matooke* (muh-TOO-kuh), steamed and mashed green bananas, make up one of the most common dishes in Uganda; bananas are also the base of a strong alcoholic liquor. Ugandan Asians also brought their style of cooking to the region, and popular Asian dishes include curries;

Kifuligo Mayido

Kifuligo mayido *(kih-foo-LEE-goe muh-YEE-doe) is made by the Adhola people of southeastern Uganda.*

You will need:

> *8 ounces (240 grams) peanuts*
> *4 cups (1 liter) boiling water*
> *2 small onions*
> *3 large tomatoes*
> *any other spare vegetables or greens*
> *salt and pepper to suit taste*

Shell the peanuts and grind them up finely, using a pestle and mortar or a food processor. Add the boiling water.

Chop the onions and tomatoes and slice up the other vegetables. Mix them with the peanut sauce in a pan and add salt and pepper to taste. Simmer lightly for about 20 minutes.

Serve with a slice of corn bread. This recipe serves four people.

samosas (sah-MOE-sahs), which are pastry parcels of spiced vegetables or meats; and chapatis, flat bread pancakes.

Uganda has enough fertile land to keep its population well fed in times of peace. However, the country faces many grave health problems. Average life expectancy is forty-one years for men and forty-two years for women. This low figure reflects the tragic devastation caused in Uganda by AIDS, a sexually transmitted

Children play in a back alley in a poor district of Kampala. Nearly half of Uganda's population is under fifteen years of age, and many of its children have been orphaned by AIDS.

disease. AIDS has left many children orphaned. Orphaned children are often cared for in Christian missions.

About two-thirds of Ugandans are Christian, equally divided between the Roman Catholic and Protestant faiths. Around 16 percent are Muslim. Other people follow a variety of African religions based on a belief in ancestral spirits.

Sixty-two percent of men and 45 percent of women can read and write. Similar disparity is found in many African countries where in the past girls have had less access to schooling than boys. Uganda has hardworking teachers and many good schools and colleges, but the troublesome years of the 1970s and early 1980s meant that many students missed out on an education altogether at that time. In 1997 the government launched a program to provide free elementary education. Under this program four children per family can attend any public elementary school at the government's expense.

Children at Mwiri elementary school in the Jinja district are taught health awareness. The most important item for discussion is AIDS, which has claimed many lives in Uganda.

Let's Talk Luganda

Luganda is the language of the Ganda people and is the most widely spoken of the country's Bantu languages.

oli otya? *(oh-lee-AWT-yah)*	*how are you?*
osiibye otya nno *(oe-seeb-yawt-YAH-noe)*	*good morning*
sula bulungi *(soo-lahb-LOONG-gee)*	*good night*
weebale *(wee-BAH-lae)*	*thank you*
nsonyiwa *(sohn-YEE-wah)*	*I'm sorry*

Languages and Peoples

Forty-six different languages may be heard in Uganda. English is still used by government, the communications media, businesses, and in secondary education. Swahili (swa-HEE-lee), the language of the eastern African coast, is widely understood and used as a second language. In Uganda it has long been the language used by the army and police.

Speakers of Bantu languages include the Ganda, Nyankole, Soga, Chiga, Nyoro, Gisu, and Toro peoples. The Ganda are the largest ethnic group. They occupy the region from Lake Kyoga (KYOE-gah) down to the Tanzanian border, including the northwestern shores of Lake Victoria. The Ganda are chiefly farmers, growing cotton, bananas, tobacco, and corn and raising cattle, goats, and chickens. Many are office

554

Villagers of Nakaseke, in the Luwero district, collect water from their new water pump. A supply of clean water is crucial to good health throughout rural Africa.

workers or civil servants. Ganda social life is based around the family and clan, with fathers holding great power within the household. Admired values are practicality, self-sufficiency, and a stoical outlook on life. There is an old custom of preparing Ganda children for adulthood by fostering them out to other families. The ceremonial Bugandan monarchy, restored in 1993, is a focus of cultural identity and pride. Many Ganda are Christian, but African beliefs are also practiced.

The Nyankole (yahn-KOE-lee), or Nyankore, people live in the region to the east of Lake Edward, where they fish, raise cattle, and grow plantains, millet, and sweet potatoes. The Soga (SOE-gah) people live in southeastern Uganda, and their homeland is called Busoga. They have always grown much the same crops as the Ganda, and the men often work on plantations, growing cash crops such as cotton and coffee.

Saints of the Shrine

Ganda beliefs centered upon a single lord of creation called Katonda, who was honored at special temples around Buganda. Humans who achieved great deeds when alive might become lubaale *(loo-BAH-lae), or saints. They too had their own shrines and were served by a priest or priestess who made offerings or told fortunes. Each Ganda saint presided over a special area of human concern. For example, Mukasa looked after prosperity and harvests, while his wife, Nalwanga, assured fertility. Other saints warded off natural disasters, such as smallpox or earthquakes.*

A youth from southwestern Uganda pushes a heavy sack on a homemade wooden scooter. Without motor vehicles, most Ugandans have to improvise to get around.

In the far southwest of Uganda, the Chiga (CHEE-gah), or Kyiga, people inhabit the highlands and lakeshores, growing millet, sorghum, sweet potatoes, and corn. Bugisu, homeland of the Gisu (JEE-soo) people, is on the slopes of Mount Elgon (EL-gahn). Its soils are very fertile, and Bugisu has long produced the best coffee in the country.

The Nyoro (uhn-YOER-oe) people inhabit the western plateau region, around the shores of Lake Albert. They live in scattered settlements, with homes clustered around a compound. Most Nyoro are small-scale farmers. They were at first chiefly cattle herders, but a hundred years or more of cattle diseases forced a change in their economy. Nyoro society has a rigid class structure. There is a royal clan, which appoints regional chiefs, who are superior to all others.

Three percent of Ugandans are Toro people, whose historical kingdom was formed when it broke away from Bunyoro. The Toro live in the far west, south of Lake Albert, and live a very similar life to the Nyoro. The land they farm includes highland as well as lakeside regions.

Straddling Uganda's border with Rwanda in the southwest live speakers of Kinyarwanda (see RWANDA). Other peoples speak languages originally from Sudan and the lands to the northeast. They include the Karamojong, Iteso, Lango, Acholi, Adhola, Alur, and Kakwa peoples.

Several ethnic groups make up the Karamojong (KAHR-moe-zhawng) peoples. The dry northeastern region where they live is called Karamoja. The Karamojong suffered terribly during a series of severe droughts in the 1980s, and many died of hunger.

To the Karamojong, cattle are very important, providing milk and blood for drinking as well as meat. Ownership of

Magic and Mystery

Many of the Nyoro are Christian or Muslim, but ancient beliefs in spirits are still strong. The ghosts of dead ancestors and relatives are believed to possess living people. They need to be pleased if they are not to do harm, perhaps by offerings or the sacrifice of a chicken. Healers may be needed to undo the spells of witches. If people have problems, a throw of cowrie shells will be used to see into the future and advise a plan of action.

cattle has great status value, and a prospective groom must give large numbers of animals to a bride's family before the wedding can go ahead. Only adult men herd the cattle, wandering in search of adequate pasture and water.

The Karamojong homestead provides a permanent base for the family. A typical homestead is surrounded by high palisades and thorn enclosures to protect against attack either by wild animals or cattle raiders. Karamojong women, elderly men, and children remain at home. The women grow sorghum and millet or gather roots and other wild foods such as termites. The termites are trapped in their towering earthen nests (a common sight all over Africa) and roasted. Children look after the herds of goats. Karamojong women normally wear a skirt of hide and many stranded necklaces. They may go bare

Karamojong women wearing bracelets, beads, and colorful wraps make bricks from red clay and dry them in the hot sun of the northeastern region of Uganda.

breasted or wear a cloak around their shoulders, held together at the front by a knot. The men may wear a long cloth wrap tied over one shoulder or go naked.

The Iteso (ih-TAE-soe), or Teso, people live southwest of the Karamojong peoples, in the fertile lands toward Lake Kyoga. Many Iteso grow cash crops, principally cotton and coffee. Women work in the fields. Iteso society is formally divided into clans and age sets. The area north of Lake Kyoga is also home to the Lango, another farming people.

The Acholi speak languages related to the Luo (LOO-oe) language of Kenya (see Kenya) and live in north-central Uganda. Acholi women grow the crops (mostly millet) while the men raise cattle. Close relatives of the Acholi include the Alur (AH-loor) of the northwest and the Adhola (ah-DOE-lah), or Jopadhola, who settled in the southeast about five hundred years ago.

Three Days with the Hairdresser

A young Karamojong warrior takes great pride in his appearance, matting his hair with red ochre and grease and shaping it into a long bun at the back of his head. After he has been initiated into manhood by spearing an ox, the bun is made into a kind of headdress. This can take up to three days to prepare. Upright rows of pegs are worked into the hair in order to hold a crest of ostrich plumes. The surface of the bun is covered with a shell of hard clay, which is then painted with patterns. The patterns vary from one tribe to another. A warrior may carry a wooden headrest, which he uses to support his hairstyle while he sleeps.

The Lugbara (loog-BAH-rah) farm the plateaus and ridges of northwest Uganda and across the border into Sudan. They grow sugarcane, pumpkins, peas, sorghum, and bananas and raise cattle. Some are Christian, some Muslim.

The Kakwa (KAHK-wah) people live in the far northwest, on the border with the Democratic Republic of Congo. They are mostly farmers, living in small villages and growing corn and millet.

Arts and Leisure

Traditional Ugandan musical instruments include drums, horns, and harps. Dances vary from one people to another and often involve groups of dancers in lines or circles. Some are accompanied by

Karamojong girls attend a cattle-blessing ceremony. The marks painted on their faces show that they are members of the Giraffe clan.

drumming, shouting, or singing. Dances may mark rites of passage, such as coming-of-age, weddings, or funerals, or may be associated with hunting, the coming of the rains, or honoring a chief or king. Dancers may wear special costumes such as leopard skins or carry shields and spears.

Uganda has a long tradition of producing arts and crafts. Basketry, black pottery, and woven cotton were of the finest quality. Wooden masks were made for rituals, and ancestral figures were carved from wood. Metalworkers produced figures of animals and birds, mostly in copper.

Woven baskets are stacked up for sale at an outdoor market in the foothills of the Ruwenzori (roo-wuhn-ZORE-ee) Mountains in far western Uganda.

Many of today's Ugandans continue to practice these crafts, but others have applied their talents to painting, textile crafts, fashion, drama, and poetry. Modern popular music has arrived from Kenya and the Democratic Republic of Congo, and the rhythmic sounds fill the markets. Ugandans love sports, too, and wherever there is a patch of grass, Ugandan boys play soccer.

Cloth Made from Bark

Bark cloth is made in many parts of Africa, but Uganda has always been a major center of production. At one time the Ganda produced fifty different grades of cloth, with the very best reserved for the kabaka himself. The finest bark in Africa comes from the Natal fig tree, which is specially cultivated for this purpose. A single section of brown bark is peeled away from the lower trunk. The tree is then wrapped with leaves to protect it while the new bark grows. The cut bark may then be soaked or wrapped in banana leaves and steamed until it is moist and yellow. It is then brought to a shed and placed over a tree trunk, where it is hammered over and over again with mallets. The bark spreads out and felts together. Finally, it is dried in the sun until it turns to a reddish brown color. It may then be painted or stenciled with geometrical patterns and borders. Bark cloth is used for clothes, ceremonial robes and cloaks, hangings, and bedding.

WESTERN SAHARA

WESTERN SAHARA LIES IN NORTHWESTERN AFRICA, bordering the Atlantic Ocean.

Most of the country is flat desert with rocks and sand hills. Low mountain ranges lie in the south and northeast.

CLIMATE

Western Sahara has a hot, dry, desert climate. Rain rarely falls, but cold air from the Atlantic Ocean produces thick fog and heavy dew along the coast. A hot, burning wind blows from the southern desert in winter and spring.

	Coast	Desert
Average January temperature:	56°F (13°C)	75°F (24°C)
Average July temperature:	92°F (33°C)	100°F (38°C)
Average annual precipitation:	7 in. (18 cm)	less than 4 in. (10 cm)

A Sahrawi refugee mother and her baby seek refuge at a camp run by the POLISARIO Front, the movement fighting for Western Sahara's independence from Moroccan rule.

A Country in Turmoil

The earliest inhabitants of Western Sahara were Berbers (BUHR-buhrs), the earliest known people of northern Africa. By the eleventh century C.E., an alliance of Berber tribes, including some from Western Sahara, conquered Morocco.

During the fifteenth century groups of Arabs arrived from Yemen in Arabia. At first the Arabs and Berbers clashed, but the two peoples eventually intermarried, and a new "Sahrawi" (sah-RAH-wee), or Saharan, culture developed.

During the late nineteenth century, rival European nations competed to control African lands. In 1884 Spain took control of the area as a protectorate, calling it Spanish Sahara. The Sahrawi people fought a war against Spain, and it was not until 1934 that the Sahrawi fighters were finally defeated. In 1956 the neighboring nation of Morocco became independent from France and Spain. The Sahrawi people also demanded freedom from Spanish rule, and an independence movement was formed.

The new Moroccan government claimed the right to rule the country on the grounds that it had been part of Morocco in precolonial times. Its wish to control the territory increased after valuable deposits of phosphate were found in the early 1960s. In 1970 Spain banned the independence movement, which only helped strengthen the demand for independence among many Sahrawi people. As a result, the POLISARIO Front independence movement was formed. POLISARIO Front is an abbreviation of Popular Front for the Liberation of Saguia el Hamra and Rio de Oro, the Spanish names for the northern and southern regions of Spanish Sahara.

In 1973 another neighboring country, Mauritania, argued that the country should become part of its territory. In 1975 the International Court of Justice said that neither Morocco nor Mauritania should have sovereignty over Spanish Sahara.

In 1975 King Hassan II, ruler of Morocco, led 350,000 unarmed Moroccan citizens into

---

FACTS AND FIGURES

Status: *Disputed territory*

Capital: *El Aaiún*

Area: *102,703 square miles (266,001 square kilometers)*

Population: *Estimated 240,000, but also over 170,000 refugees living in Algeria*

Population density: *2 per square mile (1 per square kilometer)*

Peoples: *Sahrawi (Saharan), Moroccan*

Currency: *Moroccan dirham*

Country's name: Western Sahara *describes the country's geographical location. The name was given by the United Nations in 1975.*

Spanish Sahara to stake his country's claim. The Moroccan government also encouraged other Moroccan civilians to settle in Spanish Sahara and sent Moroccan troops to occupy the towns in the north. Many Sahrawi families fled as refugees across the border to Algeria. Four huge refugee camps were set up, where today over 170,000 people live.

In 1976 Mauritania and Morocco persuaded Spain to give up control of the country. They also agreed to divide the country, now called Western Sahara, between themselves. Mauritania took over the southern third of the country. At the same time the leaders of the POLISARIO Front declared that Western Sahara was an independent state, naming it the Sahrawi Arab Democratic Republic and setting up government headquarters in Algeria. POLISARIO Front soldiers also launched

Time line:	Berbers already present	Arabs arrive from Yemen	Spain takes area as protectorate	War between Sahrawis and Spain	Moroccans occupy northeast; over 170,000 Sahrawis flee to Algeria
	1000 B.C.E.	1400s C.E.	1884	1906–1934	1975

561

POLISARIO Front fighters at their camp in the desert. Many Sahrawi men have left their wives and children for a while to join the POLISARIO Front army and fight for independence.

In 1991 a referendum was planned to ask the people of Western Sahara whom they wanted to govern them. However, nobody could agree on who should be entitled to vote.

By the year 2000 the problem of who should rule Western Sahara was still unresolved. Morocco still claims the territory, and its government runs the country on a day-to-day basis. However, the POLISARIO Front government in exile still claims the right to rule. An agreed list of voters has not been drawn up, and the referendum has still not been held.

The Sahrawis

The Sahrawi people form the majority of the inhabitants of Western Sahara. Since 1976 groups of Moroccan soldiers and workers have settled in the northern region of Western Sahara, encouraged to move there by the Moroccan government to help support its claim to the territory.

Almost everyone in Western Sahara speaks Arabic. Many people from both communities speak some Spanish as well. Both peoples belong to the Islamic faith.

Traditionally the Sahrawis were nomads, traveling across the desert from oasis to oasis in search of fresh water and grazing for their herds of camels and goats. The Sahrawis were organized into forty tribes, which provided identity, loyal support, and help in troubled times. Tribal leaders met together to solve disputes by discussion and compromise or by Islamic law. A council of male chiefs decided national policy; women did not hold public

guerrilla attacks against Moroccans and Mauritanians.

By 1979 the pressure from POLISARIO Front attacks was so great that Mauritania gave up claims to Western Sahara. Morocco did not. During the 1980s the Moroccans built a huge sand and rock wall across the desert, separating the northwest region from the rest of Western Sahara. The wall was designed to keep out the POLISARIO Front guerrillas, to mark out the area of Moroccan settlement, and to protect the Moroccan-run phosphate mines.

In 1990 United Nations troops were sent to Western Sahara to help keep the peace.

Spain gives up country; Mauritania occupies south; POLISARIO Front launches attacks against Moroccans and Mauritanians	Mauritania gives up claims	POLISARIO Front continues fight against Morocco	UN peacekeeping troops arrive; dispute over control of country unresolved
1976	**1979**	**1980s**	**1990s**

positions. However, in recent years, so many women have been left alone while men fight in the POLISARIO Front army that they have had to take over many important roles, especially in education and welfare.

Since the 1960s, when phosphate mining began, patterns of work and sources of income have been changing. However, 50 percent of the working population are still nomadic herders; a few seminomads grow fruit and vegetables at oases in the desert and on irrigated land close to the capital, El Aaiún (EL ah-YOON). In the 1980s droughts forced some Sahrawis to move to towns in the northwest region, behind the Moroccan sand wall.

Western Sahara is potentially a wealthy country. Along with its enormous deposits of phosphates, used for fertilizers and in the chemical industry, rich deposits of uranium and other valuable minerals have been found in the desert but have not yet been exploited. The cold, deep ocean waters along the coast are one of the world's best fishing grounds. Good quality ocean fish, such as tuna, are caught and canned.

Western Sahara cannot grow enough food to feed all the people living there. All luxury foods and many basic foodstuffs, such as rice, sugar, tea, and coffee, have to be imported, along with fresh water for drinking. Among the nomad Sahrawis, everyday foods are very simple. Typical foods include bread, milk, yogurt, dates, and a few fruits or vegetables from oases. Roast meat is a luxury for special occasions only. Moroccan settlers and soldiers in towns prefer to cook typical Moroccan food (see MOROCCO). The most popular drinks are tea and coffee.

A harsh climate, a poor diet, unsafe water supplies, and recent wars make Western Sahara an unhealthy place to live. Average life expectancy is forty-eight years for men and fifty-one years for women. Education is also limited, although large schools are attached to the refugee camps in Algeria.

The nomadic Sahrawi people own few large or fragile possessions. The most important crafts are weaving and carpet making. The Sahrawis use woven cloth for long, loose robes, tents and bags, and for veils to keep out the desert sand. Stories and songs entertain nomad travelers in their tents or by campfires. Storytellers and family elders also preserve the history of their tribes. The Sahrawis have a saying, "Each old person who dies is like a library that has disappeared."

Young children sing and dance at school in a refugee camp run by Sahrawi women. Although they are exiled from their homeland, Sahrawis are eager to maintain their culture.

ZAMBIA

Zambia is a large, landlocked nation in south-central Africa.

Most of the countryside is a high, rolling plateau of savanna grass and thorn trees, from 3,000 to 4,500 feet (914 to 1,372 meters) above sea level. Deep river valleys cut across the plateau. Valley soils are good for farming. In the far south the Victoria Falls, about 350 feet (100 meters) high and 1.2 miles (2 kilometers) wide, mark Zambia's border with Zimbabwe.

CLIMATE

Zambia's height above sea level means that the weather is never extremely hot, except in the river valleys. The rainy season lasts from November to April, when there can often be violent storms.

Average January temperature: *85°F (29°C)*

Average July temperature: *70°F (21°C)*

Average annual precipitation:
in the north: *48 in. (122 cm)*
in the south: *33 in. (84 cm)*

Early Settlements

Zambia (ZAM-bee-uh) has a long history of human settlement, going back to between about 40,000 and 20,000 B.C.E. Throughout the thousands of years of the Stone Age, small, family-sized groups of people roamed the country, hunting animals, collecting berries and grains, and digging for roots. Between about 100 and 300 C.E., small groups of ironworking farmers began

Pupils learn how to tell time at a Zambian village school, which has a thatched roof and is open to the weather. Many schools in Zambia have no money for books or equipment.

moving into the area from the north. They are believed to have spoken early forms of the Bantu (BAN-too) family of languages. They traded and intermarried with the hunters and gradually absorbed them into their village settlements.

By about 1000 the Bantu-speaking farmers had spread their villages throughout Zambia, and trade in iron, copper, salt, and food began to develop between neighbors. By the 1300s regular markets were held at Ingombe Ilede (ehn-GOEM-bae ih-LAE-dee), on the north bank of the Zambezi (zam-BEE-zee) River.

Zambian and Zimbabwean copper and gold were exchanged for glass beads and cotton cloth from the eastern African coast.

By the 1600s and 1700s the ancestors of many of the distinctive peoples of modern-day Zambia had settled in the region: the Luyana (later Lozi) of the upper Zambezi floodplain; the Tonga of the Toka plateau; the Bisa and Chewa in the east; and the Bemba in the north.

In about 1740 a new power emerged in the Luapula (loo-ah-POO-lah) River Valley, the Kazembe Lunda (kah-ZEHM-bee LOON-dah) kingdom. By 1800 it had become a major center of long-distance trade, selling ivory, iron, salt, and copper as far south as the Zambezi. The Bisa people acted as middlemen in the trade, while the Bemba preyed on the Kazembe Lunda trading caravans, raiding them and bringing the loot northward to sell in Tanzania.

FACTS AND FIGURES

Official name: *Republic of Zambia*

Status: *Independent state*

Capital: *Lusaka*

Major towns: *Kitwe, Ndola*

Area: *290,585 square miles (752,615 square kilometers)*

Population: *9,700,000*

Population density: *33 per square mile (13 per square kilometer)*

Peoples: *36 percent Bemba; 19 percent Tonga; 15 percent Ngoni; 8 percent Mambwe; 7 percent Lozi; more than 60 other groups*

Official language: *English*

Currency: *Kwacha*

National days: *Heroes Day/Unity Day (first Monday and Tuesday in July); Independence Day (October 24)*

Country's name: *The name Zambia comes from the Zambezi River, which forms the country's southern boundary.*

Nineteenth-Century Intrusions

In the 1830s the Kalolo (kah-LOE-loe), a Sotho people fleeing conflict in South Africa, invaded the upper Zambezi Valley. Catching the Lozi (LOE-zee) people by surprise, they took control of their kingdom. The Kalolo ruled as an aristocracy, taking Lozi women as their wives and treating the rest of the Lozi people as their slaves. In 1864 the Lozi rose up in rebellion and slaughtered all the Kalolo men. All that remained of the Kalolo was their language, which the Lozi adopted as their own.

In the 1850s the Ngoni (ehn-GOE-nee), another invading group from the south, clashed with the Bemba (BEHM-buh)

Time line:	Hunter-gatherers settle	Bantu farmers arrive	Long-distance trade develops	Ingombe Ilede is wealthy trading center	Kazembe Lunda kingdom emerges in Luapula Valley
	ca. 40,000–20,000 B.C.E.	100–300 C.E.	ca. 1000	1300s–1400s	ca. 1740

before settling in Malawi, and in about 1870 a branch of the Ngoni settled in southeastern Zambia, defeating the local Chewa (CHEE-wah). In the 1870s the first white traders from South Africa came north of the Zambezi River.

In 1889 the Lozi king, Lewanika, asked Great Britain to protect his kingdom from raids by the Ndebele (deh-BAE-lee) people to the south and to help set up schools to educate his people. Shortly afterward the wealthy South African mining capitalist Cecil Rhodes tricked Lewanika into granting mineral rights to Rhodes's British South Africa (BSA) Company. On this basis the BSA Company assumed control of the region, which they called Barotseland, and the British declared it as a protectorate (a territory under British protection).

Meanwhile, Rhodes sent agents into eastern Zambia. Most of the chiefs they encountered refused to sign any treaty of "protection." Nevertheless, Rhodes used the few treaties he did obtain to persuade the British government to declare a protectorate over what was called North-Eastern Rhodesia, to be ruled by the BSA Company. Those that resisted Rhodes's rule—the Bemba, Lunda, and Ngoni—were attacked by BSA Company troops. By the end of 1899, all of modern Zambia had been brought under colonial control.

Colonial Rule

Barotseland and North-Eastern Rhodesia were joined to form Northern Rhodesia in 1911, and in 1924 the British government took this land over from the BSA Company.

By this time large-scale copper deposits had been found in the country's center, in what was to become known as the Copperbelt, and copper mining soon became the mainstay of the colonial economy. Africans provided the labor, but they were poorly paid and forced to live in very poor housing. In the rural areas all men were forced to pay taxes in cash; often the only way to obtain cash was to go work in the mines.

By the 1950s copper prices rose and production accounted for 70 percent of Zambia's income, but most of the copper profits left the country. Royalties were paid to the BSA Company, and taxes were paid to the British government. Meanwhile, the best farmland had been set aside for white settlement, and Africans were pushed into reserves, often on poor land.

In 1953 the British joined the colonies of Northern Rhodesia (Zambia), Southern Rhodesia (Zimbabwe), and Nyasaland (Malawi) into a single federation. This was intended to benefit white settlers and to strengthen white rule. Africans opposed the move.

The first African political party in Zambia, the Northern Rhodesian African Congress (NRAC), had been founded in 1948. The NRAC organized protests, demonstrations, and boycotts of white-owned stores.

Kenneth Kaunda and others formed the more radical Zambia African National Congress (ZANC), which called for a boycott of the 1959 elections. The white government arrested Kaunda and other leaders and banned the ZANC. Kaunda's

Kalolo rule Lozi kingdom	Ngoni settle in southeast	Lozi grant the British South Africa (BSA) Company mineral rights	BSA Company rule established in British protectorates of Barotseland and North-Eastern Rhodesia	Protectorates united into Northern Rhodesia
1830s–1864	**ca. 1870**	**1890**	**1893–1899**	**1911**

Four leaders of newly independent African nations in the 1960s. Kenneth Kaunda of Zambia (left) meets Presidents Nyerere (Tanzania), Kenyatta (Kenya), and Obote (Uganda).

supporters, however, formed the United National Independence Party (UNIP), and when Kaunda was released from prison in 1960, he became the party's president. UNIP won the first majority rule elections in 1962. The British agreed to end the federation with Southern Rhodesia and Nyasaland in 1963, and Zambia became independent in 1964, with Kaunda as the country's first president.

Since Independence

Kaunda's first priority was to use his country's copper wealth to invest heavily in education, health, roads, and housing, all of which the British had badly neglected. In 1970 Kaunda's government nationalized the copper mines to use more of the copper profits for his massive government spending program. However, the economy depended too much on copper, which by then accounted for 92 percent of export earnings, and neglected agriculture.

Kaunda's plans were dealt a terrible blow in 1973 when the world price of copper collapsed, and the price of oil doubled. In addition, since 1965 Zambia had suffered from the economic sanctions imposed against the illegal white regime in Rhodesia (the former Southern Rhodesia, now Zimbabwe). Zambia could no longer use its main trade route to the sea, the railroad through Zimbabwe. Its main economic lifeline to the rest of the world was a single road to Dar es Salaam in Tanzania. A Chinese-built railroad along

Becomes British colony	Northern Rhodesian African Congress (NRAC) founded	Federation of Northern and Southern Rhodesia and Nyasaland	Zambia African National Congress (ZANC) founded	ZANC banned; United National Independence Party (UNIP) founded
1924	**1948**	**1953–1963**	**1958**	**1959**

this route was opened in 1975, but by the 1980s, when Zimbabwe won its freedom and sanctions were lifted, the Zambian economy had been crippled.

Politically, Kaunda had suppressed criticism of his government by declaring a one-party state in 1972. By the late 1980s Kaunda faced increasing criticism as people grew desperate for change. In 1991 multiparty elections were held, and the UNIP was defeated. An alliance of opposition groups won the election, and Frederick Chiluba, a former trade-union leader, became Zambia's new president. Zambia's economic crisis, however, remains very severe, poverty is spreading, and many are becoming increasingly disillusioned by Chiluba's government.

Zambia's Peoples

Zambia is home to over seventy different ethnic groups; the largest are the Bemba and the Tonga. People from different groups are not confined to particular areas of the country; in recent years many have moved around to look for work.

In the past all the Bemba were farmers who lived in small villages on the high northern plateau, where they grew grains such as millet, corn, and sorghum and root crops such as cassava. They also raised sheep and goats. Bemba society was organized in clans ruled by clan chiefs. Today many Bemba have left their villages to live and work in mining towns in the Copperbelt region and in other big cities. The Bemba play an important part in modern politics. The ruling president,

---

The Kuomboka Festival

The Lozi people of Zambia live in the deep Zambezi River Valley. Like their ancestors, many Lozi people are still cattle herders. Every year toward the end of the rainy season they move from the valley lands (which are liable to floods) to the high plains. There, they find fresh grass to feed their cattle. This annual migration is celebrated with a grand festival, called Kuomboka (kwahm-BOE-kah). Accompanied by loud drumming, the Lozi chief and elders are transported upriver in splendidly decorated canoes.

Chiluba, is a Bemba. Quarrels between Bemba and non-Bemba politicians have increased within Zambia's ruling party.

Before colonial times the Tonga (TAWNG-gah) people of southern Zambia lived as farmers, growing corn, sorghum, vegetables, and peanuts. They raised cattle and goats, caught fish in rivers and lakes, and hunted wild animals such as antelopes. Tonga society was divided into clans headed by male clan chiefs but tracing their descent through mothers and grandmothers. When British settlers came to Zambia in the 1920s, the Tonga people were driven from their villages and forced to settle on three small "native reserves." There the land was poor and infertile, making it impossible for the Tonga to grow crops. To survive, they went to work as migrant laborers on white settlers' farms

UNIP, under Kenneth Kaunda, wins first majority-rule elections	Zambian independence; Kaunda president	International sanctions against Rhodesia; Zambia loses main trade route to sea	One-party state under UNIP	Multiparty elections; Frederick Chiluba president
1962	**1964**	**1965–1980**	**1972**	**1991**

and in the copper mines of the north. In the 1950s about half a million Tonga people were forced to move yet again when the massive Kariba Dam was built on the land that was reserved for them.

Today the Tonga's chief crop is cotton; some Tonga also run cattle ranches. A few Tonga farmers are rich and own lots of land. Many others are poor and have no land of their own. They earn a living as farmworkers and artisans, making iron tools, pottery, baskets, and wooden utensils. Almost half the Tonga have moved to towns and cities, hoping to find work.

English is the official language of Zambia; it is used in government offices, businesses, mines, factories, stores, and schools. Over seventy local languages and dialects are spoken.

Christian missionaries arrived in Zambia in the nineteenth century and remain active in the country today. About 34 percent of the population are Protestant, 26 percent are Roman Catholic, and 8 percent belong to African Christian churches.

Most Bemba are Christians, but their Christian beliefs are often mixed with African religions. Bemba women make offerings to family ancestors at small household shrines; sometimes they make contact with dead chiefs and other important people by becoming "possessed" by spirits.

Most Tonga too are Christians. They often combine their faith with African

Young women use pestles (heavy sticks) and mortars (wooden bowls) to crush grain into flour. They are working close to animal pens made of woven branches.

A theater group performs a community play in a poor district of Lusaka, Zambia's capital city. Some of the actors are wearing masks in traditional styles.

beliefs. They worship a creator god called Leza and honor their ancestors and the spirits of other dead people. They believe that some of these spirits have the power to help or guide whole neighborhoods and communities and that they can be contacted by certain men or women. They also believe that people can be "taken over" by spirits called *masabe* (muh-SAH-bee), who do them harm.

A further 27 percent of the population follow purely African faiths. A small community of Muslims makes up less than one percent of the population.

An Urban Society

Zambia is one of the most urbanized countries in Africa; over 40 percent of the population lives in big cities or towns. Of these, two million people live in the capital, Lusaka (loo-SAH-kah); another two million live and work in the Copperbelt region of the north. Over the past fifty years, people have steadily drifted from the countryside

to the towns, leaving large areas of the countryside almost uninhabited.

Life for migrants to big cities is often very hard. They move there looking for work, only to find that there is no work. Many live in ramshackle shantytowns, without water and electricity. Dirt, disease, discomfort, and many kinds of crime are common. Shantytown dwellers set up small businesses in their homes, mending shoes, making clothes, hawking fruit and vegetables, buying and selling almost anything they can find. Most cities have enormous markets, lively and cheerful places, in spite of the poverty all around.

Most of the migrants to the towns are men under twenty-five years old, who leave women, children, and old people behind in the villages. Women plant crops on family plots, raise animals, care for children and sick people, and walk long distances to fetch drinking water and wood for fuel. To encourage one another and to provide companionship, they often meet together to do their daily chores, such as pounding corn into flour. Members of each village and each extended family help one another with everything from repairing houses to celebrating weddings or mourning at funerals.

The design of homes depends on the region and the people who live there. Some village houses are circular and made of mud and thatch; others are square and built of baked mud bricks, painted in bright patterns. In shantytowns people build homes of more modern building materials, such as scrap wood, concrete, and tin. Zambia's few wealthy elite live in brick, Western-style villas in pleasant suburban areas away from the noise and bustle of city centers or the squalor of the shantytowns.

Communal Dining

Most Zambian people live on simple food. Their main meal is a sticky porridge made from pounded corn, millet, or sorghum and boiled with water. It is typically served in a communal dish. Using their fingers, diners take a small lump and shape it into a ball. Then they dip the ball into a sauce made of vegetables with a little meat. Extra meat is added for special occasions, such as weddings. Grilled, baked, or added to vegetable sauce, fish is a popular food close to rivers and lakes. Fresh fruits, such as mangoes and bananas, provide dessert. Beer is a favorite drink, brewed by women from millet or other grains or made in factories and sold in bottles.

Farmworkers catch termites flying around an outdoor lamp at night. They will fry the termites in hot oil to make a tasty evening snack.

Mining Rules the Economy

For most of the twentieth century, Zambia's economy has depended on copper. It is one of the largest copper producers in the world. The country also has rich resources of cobalt, lead, zinc, coal, phosphate, and precious stones. It earns about three-quarters of its export income from these metals and minerals and also collects taxes from mining companies to help pay for running the country. Since 1970 the government has owned the largest share in all copper mines. In the 1990s international aid organizations have urged the Zambian government to privatize the mines once more to avoid waste and corruption.

Zambia is also rich in the energy needed for mining and processing minerals. Many of its rivers have been dammed to generate hydroelectric power. There are also many coal-fired power stations in the Copperbelt, producing energy for factories making chemicals, textiles, and fertilizers. Mining and other industries have led to serious air pollution and acid rain in the country's northern region.

During the 1970s copper prices fell sharply worldwide, and Zambia faced an economic crisis. Today there is a danger that some of its mines will soon be exhausted. To reduce the country's dependence on copper exports, the Zambian government has introduced projects to encourage agriculture, such as large commercial farms, growing corn, peanuts, vegetables, and tobacco. These farms mostly provide food for Zambia's large urban population, but some farm produce, especially tobacco, is exported to other countries.

Poor transportation throughout the country has hindered economic development. A long-distance railroad line, completed in the 1970s, carries goods across Tanzania to the sea, but railroad passenger travel can be slow, dangerous, and unreliable; the government does not have enough money to mend or maintain locomotives and tracks. It is almost impossible to drive on potholed country roads during the rainy season, and they are dusty and dangerous during the rest of the year.

In spite of its income from exports, Zambia remains a poor country. Recent economic problems have led to rapid inflation, which means that prices rise so fast that people cannot afford to buy essential, everyday items, such as clothes, fuel, or food.

Education and Health Care

Since independence in 1964 the government of Zambia has built many elementary and secondary schools and a new university. As a result, eight out of every ten adult men and seven out of every ten women can read and write. However, only 20 percent of the people have any secondary-level education, and only 2 percent go to college or a university.

Elementary education is free for all, but the dropout rate is high. Children often stay out of school because their families cannot afford uniforms, books, pens, and paper. There is no transportation to carry them to school, and there is a serious shortage of teachers. Parents also keep their children at home to help them earn money, care for other family members, or grow crops to survive.

Health-care services are also limited outside cities and towns. The government aims to provide free hospital care

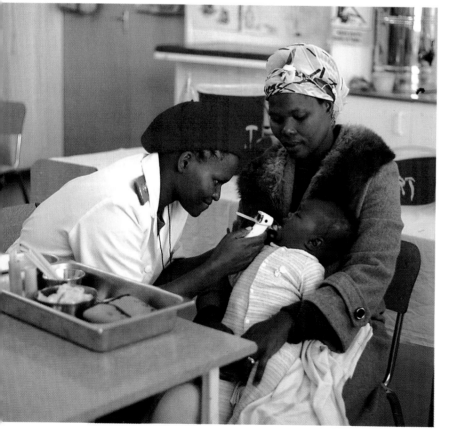

A trainee health-care worker learns how to examine a malnourished child in a training class. Malnutrition is a major problem in a poor country like Zambia.

Boys play soccer on a dusty field on the outskirts of Lusaka. Introduced in colonial times, soccer has become a popular sport throughout Africa.

and clinics for all, but Zambia has only half the trained doctors it needs and lacks the money to buy expensive medicine from Europe or the United States. Most ordinary families cannot afford doctors' fees. Instead many trust in herbal remedies or in faith healers who offer magic cures and protective charms.

Zambia faces many health problems. Polluted drinking water and inadequate sanitation mean that dangerous bacteria that cause deadly diseases can thrive. Serious diseases carried by insects are also common. The most serious threats are HIV and AIDS. One person in five is HIV positive, and three hundred new adults catch the HIV virus every day. Because of AIDS, average life expectancy is shockingly short. Both men and women can expect to survive for only thirty-seven years. The Zambian government has launched a national program to try and prevent the HIV infection from spreading further, especially among children, the country's hope for the future.

Arts and Music

A wide range of crafts are practiced in Zambia today. Zambian basketwork, pottery, and wood carving are especially fine. Baskets are woven from many different plant fibers and colored with dyes made from herbs and crushed earth. Basket makers create different designs for carrying, storage, straining beer or sieving flour, trapping fish, and serving food. They also weave mats to sleep and sit on.

Woodworkers are usually men, who make canoes, furniture, walking sticks, food bowls, drums, and masks using fine-quality timber from river-valley trees. Potters are mostly women, who shape cooking pots and dishes from natural clay and bake them in wood fires.

Music and dance play an important part in all celebrations. The most important instruments are the thumb piano; the *silimba* (sih-LIHM-bah), which is a xylophone with resonating gourds; and many kinds of drums. In cities *kwela* (KWAE-lah), a kind of rock based on South African penny-whistle music, and Western-style mambo are very popular in clubs and dance halls.

ZIMBABWE

ZIMBABWE IS A LANDLOCKED COUNTRY IN SOUTHERN AFRICA.

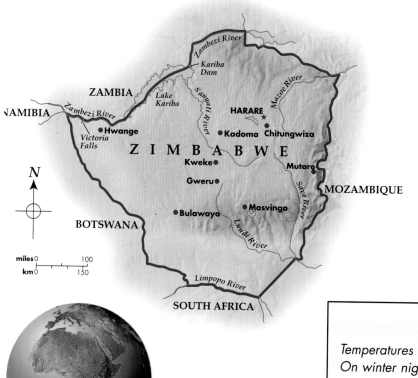

Most of Zimbabwe consists of a high, rolling plateau crossed by volcanic mountain ranges. Plateau land over 4,000 feet (1,200 meters) is known as the high veld. The Zambezi and Limpopo Rivers flow through valleys and floodplains along the northern and southern borders.

CLIMATE

Temperatures vary with height above sea level. On winter nights the mountains and the high veld can experience frost. Most rain falls from November to March. Rainfall is lowest in the semidesert southeast, where, in some years, rains fail to arrive, causing serious droughts.

Average January temperature: *65°F (18°C)*
Average July temperature: *52°F (11°C)*
Average annual precipitation: *32 in. (81 cm)*

Some of the earliest inhabitants of Zimbabwe created these images of giraffes and snakes in caves and on rocks.

From Early Settlements to Great Zimbabwe

People have lived in Zimbabwe (zim-BAH-bwae) for at least twenty-five thousand years. Probably related to the ancestors of the San (SAHN) peoples of Botswana, Namibia, and South Africa (see BOTSWANA, NAMIBIA, and SOUTH AFRICA), the earliest inhabitants were hunters and gatherers using stone tools and weapons. The first ironworking farmers arrived in the area around 100 C.E. They came from the north, probably speaking early forms of Bantu (BAN-too) languages. Because they grew their own food and kept cattle, sheep, and goats, they were able to form long-term settlements. The farmers traded and intermarried with the hunters.

By about 900 a number of changes had developed. Society began to be divided into wealthy cattle owners and commoners. Gold and copper mining were developed, especially in the western part of Zimbabwe. Long-distance trade became increasingly important, especially in gold, copper, and ivory, in the Limpopo (lim-POE-poe) Valley. Between about 1000 and 1200, this trade was dominated by a powerful state with its capital at Mapungubwe (mah-poon-GOOB-wae), a hilltop settlement in the southwest.

From about 1200 a new kingdom arose on the eastern edge of the Zimbabwe plateau. Gradually it took over the gold trade, and Mapungubwe went into decline. The capital of this new kingdom is known as Great Zimbabwe, from the Shona words *dzimba dzamabwe* (zihm-bah-zah-MAHB-

wae), meaning "stone buildings." Here, the ancestors of the modern Shona (SHOE-nah) people began building stone walls around their king's and royal family's palaces and houses. They built from local granite and constructed their walls using a dry stone-walling technique, using no mortar to hold the stones together. The largest of the stone enclosures, built between 1300 and 1400, still stands today, some 33 feet (10 meters) high, topped with beautifully shaped stone patterns. By this time Great Zimbabwe was a powerful and wealthy kingdom,

Time line:	Stone Age settlement	Arrival of early Iron Age farmers	Mapungubwe trading state flourishes	Great Zimbabwe kingdom flourishes	Mutapa and Butua kingdoms flourish
	ca. 23,000 B.C.E.	ca. 100 C.E.	ca. 1000–1200	ca. 1200–1450	ca. 1450–1670s

controlling the trade of most of present-day Zimbabwe. Eleven thousand people lived at the capital, which had become an important center for manufacturing gold ornaments and jewelry as well as weaving cotton cloth.

Massive stone walls surround the remains of a royal palace at Great Zimbabwe, built around 1300 C.E. as the capital of the Shona kings of Zimbabwe.

New Kingdoms, New Invaders

In about 1450 Great Zimbabwe was abandoned. The farmland, grazing land, and woodland were probably worn out from the activity of too large a population. The former rulers moved north and west to set up new kingdoms. To the north, in the gold-rich Mazoe (mah-ZOE-ae) Valley, they founded the kingdom of Mutapa and to the west, the kingdom of Butua, with its stone-walled capital at Khami (KAH-mee), near modern Bulawayo (boo-lah-WAH-yoe).

During the 1570s the Portuguese entered the Zambezi Valley and set up trading posts. Between 1630 and 1670 the Portuguese gained control of much of the gold mining in Mutapa, using violent methods to force people to work for them. During the 1670s a Shona military leader named Changamire Dombo drove out the Portuguese and built the powerful Rozvi kingdom that dominated most of modern Zimbabwe until the early 1800s.

In the 1830s the Ngoni (ehn-GOE-nee) from South Africa invaded the region, defeated the Shona, and sacked their capital before moving on across the Zambezi. In 1840 to 1841 the Shona suffered a second invasion from the south, this time by the Ndebele (deh-BAE-lee). The Ndebele absorbed many Shona into their ranks, and most of the eastern chiefdoms paid tribute to the Ndebele king.

Portuguese control gold mining in Mutapa	Rozvi kingdom flourishes	Ngoni invasion from south	Ndebele kingdom flourishes	British South Africa Company occupies Shona and Ndebele territory
1630s–1670s	**1670s–1830s**	**1830s**	**1840s–1890**	**1890–1893**

In the 1880s white hunters and traders from South Africa began to visit Bulawayo, the Ndebele capital. In 1888 Lobengula, the Ndebele king, was persuaded to sign what he thought was a small mining concession by the South African diamond- and gold-mining magnate, Cecil Rhodes. In fact the agreement was deliberately mistranslated for Lobengula: in reality it granted Rhodes's British South Africa (BSA) Company permission to take over the whole country.

Colonization and Liberation

In 1890 Rhodes sent several hundred well-armed men into eastern Zimbabwe. They spread out through Shona country, looking for old abandoned gold mines and taking land for farms. In 1893 BSA Company soldiers invaded the Ndebele kingdom, seizing and sacking Bulawayo, seizing all Ndebele cattle, and awarding themselves the best land in the kingdom. Both the Ndebele and Shona rose in rebellion from 1896 to 1897. Rhodes sent armed reinforcements from South Africa, and colonial control was brutally restored.

The lands of the Shona and Ndebele were formally united under BSA Company rule in 1901 as the British colony of Southern Rhodesia. By the 1920s white settlers held the best farmland, about one-third of the whole country. A further third was available for future sale to white settlers, while the remaining third, the poorest land, was reserved for Africans.

Mining soon became the mainstay of the colonial economy; gold was the most important of several minerals extracted. Africans were forced to work in the mines and on white-owned farms in order to pay heavy taxes in cash.

In 1923 the BSA Company handed over administration of Southern Rhodesia to the British government, but in practice the white settlers remained in control. Africans formed their own welfare and political organizations, but the government restricted their activities.

In an attempt to prevent African majority rule, the white settlers persuaded the British government to form a Federation of Northern Rhodesia (now Zambia), Southern Rhodesia (now Zimbabwe), and Nyasaland (now Malawi) in 1953. The settlers of Southern Rhodesia could now benefit from the wealth of the Northern Rhodesian Copperbelt and African labor from impoverished Nyasaland.

In 1961 Joshua Nkomo and others formed the radical Zimbabwe African Peoples Union (ZAPU), but the government soon banned their party. Meanwhile, whites formed an extremist political party, the Rhodesia Front, which won the 1962 elections. In 1963 the British ended the federation with Northern Rhodesia and Nyasaland. To be sure of maintaining white rule, the Rhodesia Front Prime Minister, Ian Smith, made a Unilateral Declaration of Independence from Great Britain in 1965.

While the international community imposed economic sanctions against the Smith regime, a new African party, the Zimbabwe African National Union (ZANU), sent members abroad for military

Ndebele and Shona uprisings	Southern Rhodesia is formed	Southern Rhodesia becomes self-governing colony of Great Britain	Federation of Northern and Southern Rhodesia and Nyasaland	ZAPU formed	Rhodesia Front wins elections
1896 –1897	**1901**	**1923**	**1953–1963**	**1961**	**1962**

training. After Mozambique became independent in 1975, it provided a safe haven for guerrilla armies and refugee camps. By 1979 the guerrilla armies of ZANU and ZAPU controlled most of the rural areas, and the government was forced to accept a new constitution. The first free and fair elections were won by ZANU, and Zimbabwe became independent in April 1980, with ZANU's leader, Robert Mugabe, as prime minister and, later, president.

White families watch African dancers perform at a country fair. The whites who have remained in Zimbabwe still enjoy a better standard of living than the majority of Africans.

Since independence, the Mugabe government's greatest challenge has been to correct the distorted colonial policies. Redistributing land to African peasant farmers has to be balanced against maintaining the white farming sector that grows much of the country's food and main export crop, tobacco.

In election after election Mugabe's party won almost every seat in the country's parliament. After twenty years, however, many people showed signs of wanting a change, particularly in the urban areas, where unemployment and inflation are severe problems. In the early months of 2000, government supporters violently occupied many white-owned farms and attacked and intimidated supporters of the opposition Movement for Democratic Change. The government won the general election of June 2000, but with a greatly reduced majority.

Zimbabwe's Peoples

Today the Shona make up almost three-quarters of Zimbabwe's population, outnumbering the next largest African group, the Ndebele, by four to one. Shona people control political power and hold many of the most important and influential posts in government and business.

A few smaller African groups also live in Zimbabwe, including the Sotho (SOE-toe),

ZANU formed	Ruling whites declare independence from Great Britain	War of liberation	Independence; Robert Mugabe of ZANU prime minister	Mugabe and his party remain in power; economic problems; AIDS crisis
1963	**1965**	**1966–1979**	**1980**	**1990s**

Wandering Spirits

About one year after a family member's death, the Shona hold a special ritual, called bira *(BEE-rah), to welcome the dead person's spirit, which has been wandering since they were buried, back into the family. Offerings of food and beer are taken to the grave, and prayers are said. A descendant of the dead person is chosen as the medium through whom the spirit can show its power. The family then returns home and celebrates with music and dancing. The next day, relatives sprinkle beer on a bull's head. If the bull shakes its head, this is a sign that the ancestor spirit is happy. Then there are more celebrations because the family has a new guide and helper.*

Market traders in Harare (hah-RAH-rae), Zimbabwe's capital city, sell fresh fruit and vegetables to the office workers and shoppers who are waiting for buses to take them home.

the Sena (SAE-nah), and the Tonga (TAWN-gah). Europeans form about one percent of the population, and there are about the same number of Asians.

The official language of Zimbabwe is English, used in schools, universities, and government offices. Although almost all Zimbabweans speak some English, they use Shona, Ndebele, or other African languages in their everyday lives.

About half the Zimbabwean people hold Christian beliefs, which they combine with African religions. African beliefs vary from people to people but usually involve ancestor spirits who guide and protect their descendants. Many ceremonies are designed to honor these spirits and to make contact with them. About a quarter of Zimbabweans follow African beliefs without any influence from Christian teachings.

A further 25 percent of the population follows the Christian faith alone. There are also small groups of Muslims and Hindus.

Life in Town and Country

Today about one-third of Zimbabwe's population lives in towns. Many Africans have moved to towns in search of work or to train for a career. In towns migrants without professional skills find occasional or part-time work. Big cities have suburbs of spacious, comfortable, Western-style homes, which only wealthy people can afford. Poor city dwellers live in simple, one-room houses built of rough concrete, wood, or tin.

Most African people still live and work in the countryside. Village homes are usually circular, with pointed roofs thatched with grass or straw. The walls are made of mud brick, covered with a smooth top layer of mud plaster. Groups of single-roomed houses, belonging to one large extended family, are usually arranged around a courtyard and surrounded by a wall.

Since 1980 the government has introduced plans to rebuild homes damaged during the fighting and to provide affordable housing for ordinary people in villages and towns. These modern houses are usually built of concrete blocks, with tiled or metal roofs.

A Well-Developed Economy

Zimbabwe has one of the best-developed economies in Africa. Along with mining valuable minerals, such as gold, chromium, coal, copper, platinum, and tin, it exports manufactured goods to the rest of Africa and farm products and minerals worldwide. In the early 1990s the government began to restructure its economy, aiming to encourage private businesses, reduce government spending, and control wasteful, corrupt bureaucracy. Zimbabwe needs to import petroleum but is otherwise self-sufficient in fuel. Coal-fired power stations and hydroelectric dams generate electricity.

In spite of industrial and commercial development, agriculture is still the largest sector of the Zimbabwean economy. Today one-third of Zimbabwe's farmland is owned by just four thousand families, who run large commercial farms on the best, most productive, and profitable soils. These families are mainly white, but since independence, some top-quality farms have been taken over by members of Zimbabwe's African elite.

Large commercial farms employ about 1.5 million people. Hundreds of male workers and their families can be living on each farm. The chief crops grown for export are tobacco, corn, cotton, soybeans,

Miners deep underground use powerful drills to remove lumps of rock that contain gold. The rock will be crushed and mixed with chemicals to extract the metal.

Golden brown tobacco leaves, dried in the hot sun, are one of Zimbabwe's most valuable exports. Tobacco farming and processing provide many jobs for both men and women.

fruit, vegetables, and fresh-cut flowers. Beef and ostrich are farmed for meat.

The remaining two-thirds of the farmland is divided among one million small family farms owned by Africans. Most of their farms are on poor soil, in areas of low rainfall.

Women whose husbands have gone to look for work in towns do much of the work on these farms. They grow corn, sorghum, millet, and vegetables for their own food or to sell at local markets. They also raise chickens and a few cattle. Their relatives working in towns use these family farms as a safety net to provide them with food when they can't find a job.

During the 1990s the Zimbabwean economy has been damaged by droughts, international recession, and the AIDS crisis. There is inflation and unemployment, especially among people with few technical skills. Trade unions have organized strikes and demonstrations to protest rising prices and food shortages. Zimbabwe also faces a shortage of highly skilled staff. Each year hundreds of Zimbabweans migrate to South Africa and elsewhere in search of well-paying jobs.

Food: Meat is a Treat

For most Zimbabweans the staple food is *sadza* (SAHD-zah), a porridge made from pounded corn, millet, or sorghum, served plain or with small quantities of meat or vegetable stew. Meat is a luxury; many ordinary families can afford to eat it only three or four times a month. Meat is also a sign of welcome and respect, offered to honored guests. Many different animals are eaten, including cattle, chicken, crocodile, and antelopes such as kudu and impala. Meals are served from a communal dish. Using their fingers, diners take a little piece of sadza in their right hand, then dip it in the meat or vegetable stew.

Dishes are cooked from beef reared on Zimbabwean farms. The favorite beverage is beer. In villages, women brew it for their families; in towns, it is sold in bottles. Among whites and wealthy African families, Western-style foods are popular.

Health and Education

Zimbabwe has an environment where diseases flourish. Tropical insects spread serious illnesses, and dangerous bacteria thrive in polluted water supplies. Lack of money and a shortage of trained doctors mean that medical supplies and health services are limited. In spite of these difficulties, health care for ordinary people improved after independence. Until about ten years ago, Zimbabweans could, on

Dressed in beads and feathers, a Zimbabwean healer, or n'ganga, chants and dances as he calls on the spirits of the dead to communicate with him.

Messages on Bones

An n'ganga *(ehn-GAHN-gah) is a Zimbabwean healer. His task is to promote physical, mental, and spiritual health by making peace between the everyday, visible world and the world of the spirits. He communicates with the spirits through* hakata *(hah-KAH-tah), cleaned, dried bones carved with symbols. The n'ganga scatters the hakata on the ground, then sees which symbols are visible. Each symbol has a special meaning, which he reads as a spirit message.*

average, expect to live until they were over sixty years old.

Today this is no longer true. A Zimbabwean's average life expectancy is barely forty years. Zimbabwe has the highest rate of HIV infection (the cause of AIDS) in the world. One in every four individuals between the ages of fifteen and forty-nine is HIV-positive. One-third of all babies are also born with the virus.

In the past people relied on their extended families to feed them and nurse them if they fell ill, but so many Zimbabweans have been affected by AIDS that families cannot cope. Village elders, the national government, international aid organizations, and many voluntary groups are doing their best to combat the crisis. Villages have set aside land to be

cultivated by the community to grow food for sick people and orphans. Community groups and churches organize nursing care and run orphanages.

The AIDS epidemic is also causing serious problems for the economy and changing the way people live. Active men of wage-earning age are often the first family members to catch AIDS. Many women have had to become the breadwinners for their families, as well as caring for their children, their relatives, their homes, and their family vegetable plots. Many businesses are finding it difficult to maintain a skilled workforce. They have to train three men for every job, since they know that two of them are likely to die within the next few years.

Zimbabwean people are well educated. Over 90 percent of men and 80 percent of women can read and write. After independence the government launched a campaign to improve educational facilities throughout the country. Today over two million children attend elementary school, which is free; 600,000 attend high school, and 10,000 enroll at the largest university, in Harare, every year.

Marimbas and Mbira

Music and dance are very important throughout Zimbabwe. Music played on the marimba (xylophone); *mujeje* (moo-ZHAE-zhae), which are stone bells; or mbira (ehm-BEE-rah), a thumb piano, is an essential part of many festivals and ceremonies. Everyone attending is invited to join in by singing, dancing, or clapping their hands. Mbira music is instantly recognizable: bell-like, tuneful, and full of rapidly repeating sound patterns. Often it is accompanied by complicated rhythms on gourd rattles and drums. A special, sacred, type of mbira, the *mbira dzavadzimu* (ehm-bee-rahdz-VAHDZ-moo), is played to communicate with ancestor spirits.

A young Shona man admires a massive wooden head carving. The Shona carve in both wood and stone, and stone figures have been found at the ruins of Great Zimbabwe.

Music for Freedom

Chimurenga (chee-muhr-EHNG-gah) is one of the most famous types of Zimbabwean music today. It combines traditional mbira (thumb piano) music with Western rock and jazz played on electric guitars, saxophones, and drums. Chimurenga developed during the 1970s, when the African people of Zimbabwe were fighting to remove the white-led government from power. Its name means "struggle." The most famous chimurenga musician is Thomas Mapfumo, sometimes nicknamed "the Lion of Zimbabwe." His songs have a strong political message. After performing one of them—Hokoya (hoe-KOI-yah), meaning "Watch Out"— in 1977, he was imprisoned by the white government and considered to be a dangerous enemy.

Glossary

AIDS: *a*cquired *i*mmuno*d*eficiency *s*yndrome, a normally fatal disease often passed on by sexual intercourse. It is caused by the virus HIV (*h*uman *i*mmunodeficiency *v*irus), which attacks the body's ability to resist disease and infection.

assets: valuable items such as property, businesses, or money owned by an individual, a group of people, a company, or a government.

autocratic: of or relating to ruling with unlimited authority, usually by undemocratic means.

backdrop: something in the distance, behind the main object being looked at.

baguette: a light, crispy loaf of white bread, shaped like a stick.

bureaucracy: rules and regulations governing all aspects of daily life; also, the group of people, such as government officials, who make the rules and administer them.

calabash: container made of a dried, hollow fruit, such as a gourd.

cassava: a plant with fleshy tuber roots, used as a food.

cholera: a name given to various infectious diseases marked by vomiting, diarrhea, cramps, and often death.

civil service: the officials who carry out administration work for a government, such as collecting taxes.

compulsory: enforced, often by law.

coup: a change of government brought about by force.

deforestation: the stripping of forest from the land, either as a natural process or as a result of clearance by humans, such as burning or logging.

desertification: the process of land drying up and becoming a desert.

disillusioned: disappointed.

earthworks: mounds or ditches dug from the soil to defend a place or an army.

economic sanctions: measures taken to prevent or limit trade with a particular country. The aim is to force that country to change its political system or its policies.

European Union: an alliance of European nations committed to economic union and closer political integration. It developed out of the European Economic Community (founded in 1957).

floodplain: a low-lying area that is regularly flooded by water.

genocide: the planned killing of a whole people or ethnic group.

hepatitis: one of various diseases causing inflammation of the liver.

HIV-positive: infected with the virus (*h*uman *i*mmunodeficiency *v*irus) that causes the disease AIDS.

magnate: a person of rank, power, influence, or distinction.

millet: a hardy cereal crop grown for food, drink, and fodder.

missions: centers run by people who are sent to bring a religious faith to nonbelievers. Christian missionaries often work as preachers, teachers, doctors, or nurses.

nationalize: to make something the property of the nation or state.

omen: an occurrence or sign that is believed to indicate a future event.

oust: to force from office, to get rid of.

palisade: logs planted in the ground and close together to form the walls of a fort.

plantain: a fruit similar to the banana. It is a staple food in many tropical countries.

polio: an infectious disease, often carried in polluted water. It can cause paralysis and death.

polygamy: the custom of having more than one mate or spouse at a time.

pragmatic: following policies that place practical realities before ideals.

protectorate: a territory that is given the protection of a more powerful state. In the colonial period in Africa the "protection" was often just a ploy by European countries to achieve political control of the territory.

Ramadan: the name of the ninth month in the Islamic calendar. During Ramadan, Muslims fast (go without food) from sunrise to sunset.

recession: a period of time when a country's economy is failing. During a recession, wages fall, businesses make less profit, the government is short of money, yet prices of food and other essential goods often increase.

referendum: the chance to vote on important or controversial matters.

regime: a form of government.

rehydration: replacing vital water that has been lost from a human body during sickness or great activity; replacing lost water in anything that has become too dry.

retaliate: to repay an evil deed with a similar one; to get revenge.

rigged: dishonestly operated; fixed.

savanna: a grassland dotted with trees and drought-resistant undergrowth.

show trial: a trial in which the verdict has been fixed.

smallpox: a severe disease in which the body erupts in spots.

sorghum: a grain crop commonly grown in hot countries.

subsistence farming: growing crops for one's own use rather than selling them.

trade union (or labor union): an organization of workers formed to benefit workers by trying to raise wages and improve working conditions.

tuberculosis: a disease of the tissues in the human body, especially those in the lungs.

typhoid: a disease caused by germs in polluted water. It causes severe vomiting and diarrhea.

Further Reading

Internet Sites
Look under Countries A to Z in the Atlapedia Online Web Site at
http://www.atlapedia.com/online/countries
Look under country listing in the CIA World Factbook Web Site at
http://www.odci.gov/cia/publications/factbook
Look under country listing in the Library of Congress Country Studies Web Site at
http://lcweb2.loc.gov/frd/cs/cshome.html

Togo
Akyea, E. Ofori. *Ewe.* New York: Rosen Group, 1996.

Tunisia
Brown, Roslind Varghese. *Tunisia.* Tarrytown, NY: Benchmark Books, 1998.

Uganda
See web sites mentioned above

Western Sahara
Scoones, Simon. *The Sahara and Its People.* Orlando, FL: Raintree Steck-Vaughn, 1993.

Zambia
Brown, Ernest D. *Lozi.* New York: Rosen Group, 1996.
Holmes, Timothy. *Zambia.* Tarrytown, NY: Benchmark Books, 1998.
Nwaezeigw, Nwankwo T. *Ngoni.* New York: Rosen Group, 1997.

Zimbabwe
Bessire, Mark. *Great Zimbabwe.* Danbury, CT: Franklin Watts, 1999.
Cheney, Patricia. *The Land and People of Zimbabwe.* New York: HarperCollins Children's Books, 1990.
Johnson, Robert, Jr., and Gary Van Wyk. *Shona.* New York: Rosen Group, 1996.
Schneider, Elizabeth. *Ndebele.* New York: Rosen Group, 1996.
Sheehan, Sean. *Zimbabwe.* Tarrytown, NY: Benchmark Books, 1996.
Zimbabwe. Broomall, PA: Chelsea House, 1997.

Index

Page numbers in *italic* indicate illustrations.

Page numbers in *italic* indicate illustrations.